Action at a Distance

T0168550

IN SEARCH OF MEDIA

Timon Beyes, Mercedes Bunz, and
Wendy Hui Kyong Chun, Series Editors

Action at a Distance

**John Durham Peters, Florian Sprenger,
and Christina Vagt**

IN SEARCH OF MEDIA

University of Minnesota Press
Minneapolis
London

meson press

In Search of Media is a collaboration between the University of Minnesota Press and meson press, an open access publisher, https://meson.press

Published by the
University of Minnesota Press
111 Third Avenue South, Suite 290
Minneapolis, MN 55401-2520
https://www.upress.umn.edu

in collaboration with
meson press
Salzstrasse 1
21335 Lüneburg, Germany
https://meson.press

ISBN 978-1-5179-1009-9 (pb)
A Cataloging-in-Publication record for this book is available from the Library of Congress.

The University of Minnesota is an equal-opportunity educator and employer.

Contents

Series Foreword

"Media determine our situation," Friedrich Kittler infamously wrote in his Introduction to *Gramophone, Film, Typewriter.* Although this dictum is certainly extreme—and media archaeology has been critiqued for being overly dramatic and focused on technological developments—it propels us to keep thinking about media as setting the terms for which we live, socialize, communicate, organize, do scholarship, et cetera. After all, as Kittler continued in his opening statement almost thirty years ago, our situation, "in spite or because" of media, "deserves a description." What, then, are the terms—the limits, the conditions, the periods, the relations, the phrases—of media? And, what is the relationship between these terms and determination? This book series, *In Search of Media,* answers these questions by investigating the often elliptical "terms of media" under which users operate. That is, rather than produce a series of explanatory keyword-based texts to describe media practices, the goal is to understand the conditions (the "terms") under which media is produced, as well as the ways in which media impacts and changes these terms.

Clearly, the rise of search engines has fostered the proliferation and predominance of keywords and terms. At the same time, it has changed the very nature of keywords, since now any word and pattern can become "key." Even further, it has transformed the very process of learning, since search presumes that, (a) with the right phrase, any question can be answered and (b) that the answers lie within the database. The truth, in other words, is "in there." The impact of search/media on knowledge, however, goes beyond search engines. Increasingly, disciplines—from sociology to economics, from the arts to literature—are in search of media as a way to revitalize their methods and objects of study. Our current media situation therefore seems to imply a new term, understood as temporal shifts of mediatic conditioning. Most broadly, then, this series asks: What are the terms or conditions of knowledge itself?

To answer this question, each book features interventions by two (or more) authors, whose approach to a term—to begin with: *communication, pattern discrimination, markets, remain, machine*—diverge and converge in surprising ways. By pairing up scholars from North America and Europe, this series also advances media theory by obviating the proverbial "ten year gap" that exists across language barriers due to the vagaries of translation and local academic customs and in order to provoke new descriptions, prescriptions, and hypotheses—to rethink and reimagine what media can and must do.

Introduction

Florian Sprenger and Christina Vagt

> A body is never moved naturally, except by another body which touches it. Any other kind of operation on bodies is either miraculous or imaginary.
>
> —Gottfried Wilhelm Leibniz

When Gottfried Wilhelm Leibniz in his exchange with Samuel Clarke in 1715/1716 famously attacked Newton's theory of gravity for introducing "imaginary operations" and "occult forces" into physics, he evoked the classic Aristotelian ban of action at a distance: Every motion requires a conjoined mover. No action can occur without a loss of force and thus without duration. Only by postulating some underlying medium could the effects of gravity, as well as electricity and magnetism, be conceived as contact forces or action through contact. Aristotle's dictum was translated into modern physics: Every transmission of a force from the location of its cause to that of its effect requires a medium to ensure its interaction. In the context of this debate, media were regarded as mediating instances that enabled what was called communication. If cause and effect were not immediately connected but rather spatially separated from one another—as in the case of gravitation, magnetism, or electricity, for instance—then there had to be a medium to ensure both the transmission of the force and the causal connection.

Even though it is a matter of debate if Newton believed what Leibniz attacked him for, his thinking, exemplary for modern physics, revolved around media: Newton used the terms "ambient medium," "refracting medium," or "transparent medium" (each written with lowercase letters) to refer to mechanical transmission capacities that infuse everything, leaving no empty spaces. At the same time, he used the term *medium* (both in English and Latin) when speaking about transmission media or intermediate media such as air, glass, or the ether. Clarke, as a substitute for Newton in the debate with Leibniz, summarized this necessity as follows: "Nothing can any more *Act,* or be *Acted upon,* where it is not present; than it can *Be,* where it is not" (Leibniz and Clarke 1956, 21). The spirits, ethers, and media introduced by Newton create such a material connection and in turn inaugurate, with the proximal effect explained by them, an action at a distance by means of an imperceptible medium. The intermediary is no longer simply spatial but also transmits forces such as gravitation, electricity, or light (see Spitzer 1948).

If things seem to act at a distance—if gravitation, magnetism, or electricity can overcome distances without evidencing a visible cause for doing so—then the question of the causalities, continuities, and materialities of this action gains considerable significance. Modern physics as a systematic science has to develop criteria for determining which forces are subject to a medium and which actions were simply miraculous or inexplicable. In this context, the philosophical debates about the *structure* of space and time were updated in light of their historical background and thus, as far as the present day is concerned, made legible in implicitly media-theoretical terms. They were propelled by a sense of unease about the material conditions needed for forces to be mediated over distances. For, if no force could be identified to account for such mediation, then the path was cleared for divine intervention, magic, and miracles.

In the course of the development of electrodynamic theories and technologies during the eighteenth and nineteenth centuries, physics operated successfully within the framework of Newtonian mechanics and the speculative assumption of an intermediary—the ether—as the underlying medium that acts through contact on certain bodies. But the fact that nobody had ever seen or measured it occupied physicists and philosophers alike by evoking dazzling proofs and thought experiments from Immanuel Kant to Hendrik Lorentz (see Vagt 2007). After special relativity finally abolished the ether as physical medium, Albert Einstein famously attacked the theoretical physics of Niels Bohr and others, stating that quantum mechanics with its presupposed quantum states of "superposition" and "entanglement" of particles contained some "spooky" action at a distance (see Barad 2007, 317–31). Even though these physical debates took place at different times and on different scales (macro- and microphysics) they both stress the media question concerning modern physics: How is it possible that objects interact with each other from a distance, without touching?

When physics describes how things act on each other, how objects exert forces on other objects, it has to take the materiality of transmission into account. Physics, compelled to think about media, is one of the fields of knowledge in which terms of media are forged. This book follows some of the trajectories *action at a distance* has taken from physics to questions of human interaction, the binding and breaking of time and space, and the entanglement of the material and the immaterial in physics and aesthetics. The three texts each deal with historical constellations in which the mediality of transmission and the materiality of communication are debated as questions of acting at a distance—an action, it turns out, whose agency lies in a medium. They discuss different episodes of the epistemological history of mediation, and move through different modes of causation from the immateriality of the mind to the materiality of infrastructures and follow the trajectory of the transmission of forces. The common question that brings them together deals with the conceptual history of mediation: they trace the epistemological transformations of what *mediation* (and the related terms *communication* and *causation*) means in different historical contexts. How is mediation represented and narrated, how does it challenge the boundary of the material and the immaterial, and how does it change in relation to technologies of mediation? In all three texts, the distance that mediation implies, the meanwhile, the difference and the in-between, turn out to be both the challenging and dis-unifying potential of mediation and the source of its technical implementations.

With the advent of electromagnetic telegraphy in the 1830s, a notion emerging from the history of the sciences of electricity diffused into popular knowledge: the instantaneous transmission of electric action. Ever since Stephen Gray, as described by Florian Sprenger's essay, explored the possibility of electric transmissions through copper wires in 1730, the speed of electricity was an item of interest and subject of investigation. Speed was conceived as the possibility of nonspeed, as instantaneity means to neglect speed. Instantaneity means that transmission does not take any time. Electricity and telegraphy were described as timeless and thus having no speed. There is a small difference between slow speed and no speed, but this difference means everything to physics. Because nothing can take place in two places simultaneously and because any distant effect requires a medium, the experiments that Sprenger's paper describes were stalked by phantasms of instantaneity, immediate transmission, and *actio in distans*. Simultaneity thus becomes a matter of cultural techniques of synchronization.

As John Durham Peters shows, such means of control of simultaneity—be it through knowledge, narration, or action—are deeply embedded in Western history. His text engages with a host of examples of what he calls "meanwhile structures" situated at the intersections of time and space. For knowledge and for narration, time and space are no barriers and action at a distance is a way of synthesizing them: Being at two places at the same time turns out to be necessary to narrate stories and know the world—knowledge and narration, again, have an agency that acts also at historical distances. But being at two places at the same time is only possible under the rarest of conditions: when one can work in the no-speed mode of instantaneous access of nonlinear movement. Most efforts at action at a distance are, instead, subject to the demons of microtime, who mischievously filter, distort, block, warp, or delay action at a distance.

Action at a distance through language and communication, concepts and models is typically human. German philosopher Hans Blumenberg introduced the Latin neologism *actio per distans* as a philosophical term that signifies a prominent type of preemptive action among humans: action in absence of the object that is acted upon. Christina Vagt's paper discusses this version of action at a distance in the form of concepts, models, and simulations in the field of today's biosciences, where models determine under which conditions material action takes place. When an Australian banksia cone suddenly opens its follicles after a wildfire to release its seeds, cause and effect are evident to the careful observer (the fire gets rid of the competition), but *how* something that is technically dead can perform this kind of dynamic motion does appear somehow magical—until imaging and modeling technologies finally enable the scientists to procure a viable model. Addressing the media question underlying material research in the age of computer simulation moves the discussion away from *actio in distans* and the inherent causality, instantaneity, and simultaneity debates of theoretical physics and toward aesthetic procedures that mediate between matter and mathematics and between scientists and their epistemic objects.

The term *medium,* this book argues, is—at least partly—a historical effect of the philosophical and physical challenges of actions across distance, but it also conveys a certain ambivalence: The term *medium,* Leibniz claimed, was always in danger of being used willy-nilly to explain a situation that might otherwise seem to be miraculous on account of its unknown logic, causality, or mode of operation:

> If the *Means,* which causes an *Attraction* properly so
> called, be constant, and at the same time inexplicable
> by the Powers of Creatures, and yet be true; it must be a

perpetual *Miracle*: And if it is not miraculous, it is false. 'Tis a Chimerical Thing, a Scholastick *occult Quality*. (Leibniz and Clarke 1956, 94)

Miracles, Leibniz thought, were evoked when a mediating principle was needed to explain physical phenomena without explaining their specific operations. Associated with this danger was the fact that the mediation of a physical effect could only be explained by replacing the miraculous with a medium that was itself unexplained. The mediation might have occurred in an inexplicable manner, but the medium did not appear to be miraculous because, by means of its alleged physical properties, it was more or less able to explain the phenomenon in question. Although the mediation of the medium took place in an inexplicable way, it seemed to explain one process or another by its mere introduction, and this was because media, according to the physics of the time, were defined as material connections that ensured the causality between cause and effect. To summarize Leibniz's critique: If media could be used in such a way to explain physical processes, then they served as "argumentative resources" (Cantor 1981, 152) for explaining the inexplicable while hiding, beneath the cloak of a medium of communication, the fact that the process in need of explanation was not explained at all but rather replaced by the postulation of a causal connection that was itself left unexplained. In all of its arbitrariness, the medium would thus come to acquire a sort of magical power, for it was used to explain the inexplicable simply by being mentioned—"groundless and unexampled" (Leibniz and Clarke 1956, 94). His advice is a theory of media: Never replace a miracle with a medium, and never mistake a medium for a miracle. The medium always has physical properties that mediate its actions even at a distance.

References

Barad, Karen Michelle. 2007. *Meeting the Universe Halfway: Quantum Physics and the Entanglement of Matter and Meaning*. Durham, N.C.: Duke University Press.

Cantor, G. N., 1981. "The Theological Significance of Ethers," in *Conceptions of Ether:*

Studies in the History of Ether Theories 1740–1900, ed. G. N. Cantor and M. J. S. Hodge, 135–56. Cambridge: Cambridge University Press.

Leibniz, Gottfried W., and Samuel Clarke. 1956. *The Leibniz-Clarke Correspondence.* With the assistance of H. G. Alexander. New York: Manchester University Press.

Spitzer, Leo. 1948. "Milieu and Ambiance." In *Essays in Historical Semantics,* 179–316. New York: Vanni.

Vagt, Christina. 2007. "Absolut ruhend." In *Stehende Gewässer: Medien und Zetilichkeiten der Stagnation,* ed. Butis Butis, 151–62. Berlin-Zürich: Diaphanes,.

Temporalities of Instantaneity: Electric Wires and the Media of Immediacy

Florian Sprenger
Translated by Erik Born

On a warm summer day in 1729, a copper wire was suspended across a garden in the south of England. When one end of the wire came into contact with an electrified glass cylinder at the other end, in the very same moment, little pieces of brass leaf began to dance along the wire and settled down on it like butterflies. The person who had electrified the wire was Stephen Gray, a passionate researcher and a dyer by trade. In doing so, Gray was able to create an "elecktrick virtue" (Gray 1731a, 27)—an attraction, an electric force—from one side of the garden to the other, a result confirmed only by the sound of his friend Granvile Wheler's voice and without any visual confirmation. It even sufficed to hold the glass cylinder near the wire without touching it. Sometime later, Gray would suspend a schoolboy horizontally and electrify him, in turn, with a glass cylinder, thereby making little sparks shoot out from the boy's fingertips to the onlookers. At this stage, the invisible force still did not have the power to decide over matters of life and death, even if it could already be used to kill small birds. It was still not possible to distribute anything more than undifferentiated sparks, or even to charge them with meaning and code. Transmission was still entirely without meaning or application—a medium without a message, or rather, a medium whose message consisted in the fact that it existed, that it had an effect where there should be none. The wire filled a distance, a space between cause and effect, with its materiality. Electric action transmitted through the wire seemed to be instantaneous, simultaneous, immediate.

And it communicated. Gray called the wires "lines of communication" (Gray 1731a, 27). He did not have a concept like "cable" at his disposal. He knew nothing of insulation, states of electrical charge, or electrons. Communication, for the physical knowledge of his times, meant the connection between cause and effect. Between them, a transmission took place: the necessity of a causal link. Every process in the universe, according to the physics of the time, must have a cause from which it can be explained. For electricity to be able to "communicate" in this sense, three conditions are necessary: two separate elements communicating, one at each end, and an in-between. The transmitter and the receiver have to differ from each other, or else there would be no channel and no connection. There have to be "two" in order for there to be a "one." However, these two require a "third": the medium. Communication presupposes a difference, an abyss between sender and receiver (see Peters 2000 and Chang 1996). Connection requires separation. The aim of communication, speaking generally, is to overcome this temporal or spatial difference, to make it disappear. Yet, electricity does not merely jump across this abyss; in Gray's experiment and in many other instances of the sciences of electricity, it appeared to eliminate this abyss entirely. The transmission of electricity displaces space and makes temporal differences imperceptible, thereby leaving both space and time immeasurable, while also inserting a piece of wire into them. Although cause and effect had been separated from each other, they still appeared to be simultaneous—and connected through a lengthy copper wire.

Gray was not able to say whether electricity has a speed. To him, it appeared not to require any mediation or any code. It was just there, appearing simultaneously at both ends of the channel, which was consequently no longer a channel but still opens up a space between seemingly simultaneous events. The people communicating over the wire did not have to be present at the same place to be connected. But their present coincides. What happened on Gray's end of the cable appeared to happen at the same time on Wheler's end of the cable. Between the ends of a cable, there can be an entire garden—soon, the entire world, measured out in copper wire—but there can be no minute, no second, no moment, no blink of the eye, no delay. The cable and its communication lead to an investigation of communicability itself. It spans gaps, and, as a medium, it is presupposed by the connection. What Stephen Gray transmitted in that garden in the south of England in the summer of 1729 was transmissibility; what was communicated in this communication was communicability.

The Materiality of Temporality

Cables connect the world. They are everywhere—crossing, branching, and interconnecting—wherever electricity, whether as energy or signal, should be conducted. Our world is universally connected and linked together, on a small scale as on a large scale. Cables are hidden inside every housing, behind every wall, in every ocean. Whether overground or underground, they connect cities and settlements, continents and colonies. As ubiquitous as cables may be in our current media-saturated world, rarely do they come into view, so concealed is their history.[1] So inconspicuous as to be frequently overlooked, the cable, as a medium underlying other media, can contribute to our understanding of our own time and its spaces. Its history is a history of connections and disconnections, of temporalities and spatialities, and it involves a history of mediation and of immediacy. Thus, the history of the becoming of cables to be told here is a history of the overcoming of distances in durations so short that they are deemed nonexistent, though mediation depends on them. The media history of the cable is a history of the phantasm of immediacy.

Cables, as Nicole Starosielski (2015) has shown, carve up geographic and architectonic spaces, but they are localizable and limited. They overlay geographies and architectures with their own relations by redefining places in terms of the beginning or the end of a material link. The interconnection of cables creates new "spaces of address," a collection of all the distant places that can be reached from a single place, medially, via cable. In different historical stages, these "spaces of address" are developed with technical means of connection and disconnection from cable networks over wireless transmissions to digital networks. The basic fact, though, remains constant: The cable addresses because it connects. From the time of Gray's experiments on, the history of the cable is bound to the history of addressing (see also Peters 2006). The cable creates a relation between transmitters and receivers, be they human or technical, thereby bringing about their addressability, perhaps even their identity (Siegert 1999), though at the very least their ability to be spoken to in that they bear an address. Every cable has a beginning and an end, and with that, a goal in and of itself.[2] The materiality of the cable, with its two ends, implies two addresses. Transmitter and receiver are functions of the cable, and consequently, writing this history implies writing the history of these addresses, even before they turn into a network. If every hardwired transmission implies a destination, this place is located at the end of a cable.

Since that summer in 1729, cables span the world due to two main improvements. The first was in terms of the amount of time that passes during a transmission. Transmission time is extremely quick, supposedly even instantaneous. Eventually, significant debates in physics will revolve around its duration. The second was that the cable establishes a material connection between the places at the two ends of the cable. Laying a cable does not merely open up a space; it also connects points in space. A cable is never only "here," but always also "elsewhere."

Consequently, from the perspective of media studies, the cable makes evident the phatic level of the relation between transmitter and receiver—the fact that there will always be a channel between them before there is any message. The materiality of the cable influences what can be transmitted "over the wire." It organizes space and time in that it separates transmitter and receiver, spatially and temporally. The cable itself contains a dimension of connection. Disturbances of the cable make it into the object of research, generating knowledge about its potentials including charge, delay, and transmission (see Hunt 1994). The space and time and the phantasms bound to this first electric medium are the subject of this essay.

Sciences of Electricity, Practices of Wiring

At the time of Gray's experiments, electricity was commonly understood as an attribute of objects that would attract other objects after being heated or rubbed (see Heilbron 1979). Accordingly, the concept of electricity designated a quality that had to be produced through manual labor. Interest in electricity was focused on researching corpuscles and effluvia, the smallest little bodies that were imagined, according to the most widespread mechanistic theories, to mediate electric and magnetic effects. Space, so people assumed, was filled with these imperceptible bodies, which were the cause of every effect, every phenomena, including that of electricity. Although electricity would gradually emerge as a well-defined field of study, it was not institutionalized for the time being, since the results of experiments with electricity were too dispersed and the uses of electricity too vague, hardly extending beyond spectacular experiments with illuminating balls, floating brass leaves, and sparking glass—all of which was an end in itself. Responsible for this delay were the precarious and unclear status of electricity and the insignificance of electric phenomena. Nobody "mastered" electricity; producing it demanded a lot of talent, dexterity, and patience (Schaffer 1997, 464).

The rules for making electric phenomena appear were largely rules of instrumentation. In the experiments conducted by William Gilbert around 1600 or Francis Hauksbee around 1710, which had marked out the field of electricity before Gray, all the components in the experimental setup were located within a single room and they all had to be visually perceptible. With Gray, however, the framework changes: the spatial "co-presence" of a "transmitter" and a "receiver" is no longer necessary. Attraction no longer takes place where the electrified objects are located, as in the model of attraction discussed in the context of magnetism. If electricity itself can be transmitted and "communicated," as Gray's experiments would subsequently suggest, then the site of its production would no longer necessarily be identical with that of its effect. Electricity, it turns out, can be sent and transmitted. To do so, wires have been bent, hung, compressed, extended, and knotted in a variety of forms.

Substances of Communication

The path from the wire to the cable leads through several detours. As early as 1708, Gray had written a letter to Hans Sloane, the secretary of the Royal Society, the most influential scientific institution of its time. As a simple craftsman, Gray did not have the privilege of access to the expensive instruments of the Royal Society, falling back instead on simple glass tubes, feathers, and brass leaves. In the letter, Gray describes how he made a glass tube, which had been electrified by rubbing it, attract a down feather at a distance of a meter—nothing less than a world record in terms of electrical action at a distance:

> If when the feather is come to the Glass it be held at about 6 or 8 inches Distance from the side of a wall edge of a Table Arme of a Chair or the like it will be drawn to it and thence to the Glass again and that for 10 or 15 times together without ceasing it flies to object at a greater Distance but then does not soe often Return. (quoted in Chipman 1954, 34)

Gray's unpublished letter lays the theoretical foundation for the
space and time of transmission that the cable will come to occupy.
In the letter, he sets himself the challenge of explaining how
effluvia that have been made to radiate outward due to rubbing
can attract things back to themselves. However, Gray is unable to
present a solution to this problem of attraction. He even tries to
refer back to phenomena of repulsion, which had long fallen out of
the typical framework of observation:

> When the feather is come to the Glass and thence Reflect-
> ed if you follow it with the Glass twill flee from it and will
> by noe means be made to touch it till driven near to the
> next wall in the Room or some other solid object by which
> twill be attracted and freely return to the Glass again
> Repeating its Reflections. (quoted in Chipman 1954, 35)

Whenever the feather touched the glass, according to Gray, it was
repelled first to the bodies surrounding the glass, and would only
then come back to it. Gray's conjecture here was that all bodies
emit effluvia, mutually interacting with one another (see Heilbron
1979, 234), and his later view would be that these effluvia transmit
so much electric force through the air that any receiving objects
would likely become electric. Since these effluvia were imagined
to be something like an atmosphere surrounding an object, they
should have affected any surrounding object. As the effluvia were
flowing outward, any surrounding body was also supposed to become temporarily electric: "as all bodies Emitt soe they Receive part
of the Effluvia of all other bodies that Inviron them and that the
attraction is made according to the current of these Effluvia" (quoted in Chipman 1954, 36). For Gray, this exchange of smallest bodies
fills the entirety of space and creates a network out of effluvia flowing between separate objects. In this conceptual framework, there
is immediately a connection between anything that winds up within
electricity's sphere of influence. This space is open but it extends
only a few centimeters.

How do objects become electric beyond a distance of several centimeters, Gray was asking himself, without touching? How do things,

whether glass tubes or planets, have an effect at a distance? This question was central to physics since Aristotle, who put forward the principle that there must be spatial and temporal contact between cause and effect (Aristotle 2008; see Hesse 1955). If a cause and an effect are related to each other in spite of the distance between them, then they have to be connected by a medium. As a tenet of medieval Aristotle reception has it, "Every action happens through contact, which is why nothing acts at a distance, unless through some medium" (*Omnis actio fit per contactum, quo fit ut nihil agat in distans nisi per aliquid medium*).[3] In this economy of causality, an *immediate* effect at a distance, relating two places to each other without time, is strictly forbidden. To circumvent this prohibition and to explain phenomena like electricity and magnetism, various media have been introduced as "argumentative resources" (Cantor 1981, 152), including ethers, spirits, corpuscles, or effluvia. These media ensure continuity even at a distance, conjuring up a connection even without contact—*actio in distans.*

Gray's experiments also followed this powerful theoretical guideline of the physics of that time, though he would be the first to build an electric medium. However, his theses about attraction and repulsion did not initially find any resonance. His next publication would appear only twelve years later, an interim during which he worked in the laboratory of Newton popularizer John Theophilus Desagulier. After another ten years of silence, Gray's publications and influence began to build. In 1731, he demonstrated his experiments to the Prince of Wales, whom Desagulier served as the court physician, and the Royal Society awarded him with the first ever Copley-Medal, which is still given out today, and did so again in the following year. Gray's work was part of a larger change in scientific practice—a movement toward professionalization that would have challenged his authority as a poor dyer had his experiments been conducted only a few decades later. However, it was precisely this manual dexterity, "the dyer's knack," (Schaffer 1997, 464) that was decisive for the success of his experiments. As the historian of science Simon Schaffer has shown, Gray's exceptional dexterity enabled him to conduct many experiments that would have been difficult for those lacking in practice.

Action at a Distance

Gray's first, short published statement about electricity of 1720, though not influential in the scientific community, opens with an important observation. After conducting several experiments with glass tubes and a down feather attached to a stick, Gray had come to a crucial realization: even without the glass tubes, the feather would still be attracted to the stick, "as if it had been an Elecktrick Body, or as if there had been some Electricity communicated to the Stick or Feather" (Gray 1720, 104-5). Gray's precise description of the phenomena of charge and discharge, which at the time were still not defined as such, was the precondition for his thesis that electricity can be made communicable. The focus of his research changes here from attraction to transmission—namely, transmitted attraction—and thus continues the concern with electrification at a distance that the published letter only hints at. Among the objects Gray was able to electrify was himself, as his fingers attracted feathers or hair. At first, Gray was working with threads and paper, "finding them, after they had been well heated before rubbing, to emit conspiciously their Elecktrick Effluvia" (Gray 1720, 106). If many effluvia gather together, Gray thought, they could be passed on through communication, without any corresponding loss or exchange.

In his next report, published in 1731 though referring to events of 1729, Gray begins with a mention of more experiments with glass tubes, but then, after several changes of scene, goes far beyond them, and describes electricity in terms of transmission (Gray 1731a). At this moment the cable takes the stage. To prevent dust from entering the open tubes, which were about a meter long and a few centimeters wide, Gray had stopped them up with pieces of cork. To his surprise, the corks at the end of the tubes did not change the effect of the tube, but precisely the opposite: the corks themselves proved to be attractive. In the prevailing order of science, this should have been impossible, since the corks themselves were not electrified.

At first, Gray was not studying action at a distance but action close up, an effect that would be explained today as "induction." He went on to replace the corks with all kinds of other materials, or he would touch these materials to the corks, thereby transferring electricity from one object to the next without having to rub it. Consequently, the cork became a carrier, whereas the transmission, in previous experiments, had occurred through effluvia in space. Gray was able to transmit electricity from one object to another, even if a wire was attached to a cork perpendicularly. In this manner, diverse objects could be attached to the tubes hanging in the air, and together they formed a new kind of experimental setup. The space of transmission now reached, with the cable, from the tube to the object.

This is precisely why Gray was able to electrify things—because he did not intentionally touch them with his hand, as had always happened up till then. In Gray's setup, objects are, to use our current terms, "isolated against discharge." First, several materials had to be constructed as a continuous line. If the effect (which had only been present where something had been electrified) appears now at the end of the experimental setup, then the object in the space between can also be electrified, and it should function as a suitable carrier. The in-between object becomes the medium of communication. Gray would try out diverse carriers of communication, such as a fishing spear made of Spanish cane, stovepipes, fireplace tongs, as well as whale bones and other sticks or rods, copper and iron wire, cords, a tea kettle, even vegetables. Since the transmission works best with copper wire, the questions arise as to the maximum possible length of this kind of conductor, and the potential distances it might overcome—an early signal range test, as it were.

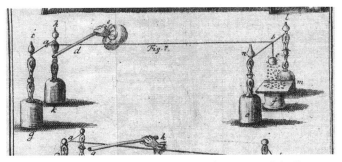

[Figure 1.1]. Gray's Cable. Source: Johann Gabriel Doppelmayr, *Neu-entdeckte Phaenomena von bewunderswürdigen Würckungen der Natur* (Nürnberg: Fleischmann, 1744), Table II.

How these pieces of wire were connected to each other is not mentioned in any of Gray's reports. At the time, production methods made it possible to create pieces of wire that were at most a few meters long, and these could then be tied to each other to increase the overall transmission distance. However, Gray was not interested in finding a practical use for his experiments. They are not precursors of telegraphy, however much they may be appear to be. After proving that a certain range was attainable, Gray did not continue the experiments. Although a transmission distance larger than a few hundred feet appears to have been theoretically possible, Gray initially had no desire to test it. Alongside the fascination with attraction without a visible cause, there was also fascination with action at a distance that would eventually overcome distances too great for the eye to see. There are spatial limits to this desire. At first, only a few meters. For longer experimental setups, Gray's room was too small. His first experiments with a horizontal suspension failed, because he was using the same material for attaching things and as a conductor. Only a trip to the countryside in Ottenden Place in the county of Kent, in the presence of his friend Granvile Wheler, a clergyman and Fellow of the Royal Society, allowed Gray to continue his research in spaces larger than those of his room in the city, and subsequently to present them to the public of the Royal Society upon returning to London.

Electricity in the Garden

Gray's accounts of these garden experiments show the significance of narrative patterns for anchoring epistemic innovations. What could be more unlikely, in this idyllic setting, than the annihilation (or, at the very least, manipulation) of space and time? Since no one from the Royal Society was able to be present for the experiments, Gray's narration made the reader of the *Philosophical Transactions* into a virtual witness. Gray and Wheler began by hanging the tubes vertically, which would then attract brass leaves lying on a wooden stool or a glass pedestal. They were able to continue this sequence by attaching other materials to the tubes and introducing a rod with a piece of ivory at the bottom end. Since Wheler's house was equipped with a balcony and even a clock tower more than ten meters high, they were able to experiment with longer setups, yet even this height was not enough to exhaust the effect. For his return to London, Gray planned to hang a tube from the highest point of the cupola of St. Paul's Cathedral, which would have then attracted a brass leaf in the altar sanctuary. However, this plan proved unnecessary when Wheler proposed attaching the conductor to the roof and having the setup proceed horizontally rather than vertically. The advantage of the horizontal setup was that no disturbance was possible through "discharge" on any sup-porting object, which could itself be a conductor, though not in the right direction. Gray did not supply a reason for this hypothesis, which would become enormously important for further electricity research.

Only after several trials did it turn out that the decisive factor was not the thickness of the carrier but its material composition. The experiment succeeded only with silk threads as suspension. This discovery was crucial because insulation—which Gray was still not able to name as such—makes of a wire something more than it is: the wire becomes a cable. Insulation is the necessary condition of the cable, since nothing will flow through an uninsulated wire, and the wire will not function as a carrier. The shift in Gray's experiment from a copper suspension to silk threads implies a distinction be- tween conductors and nonconductors, and, with that, a description of insulation in which the wire turns into a cable. As Gray describes the experiment,

> Then the Cane being rubbed, and the Leaf-Brass held un-
> der the Ivory Ball, the Electrick Vertue passed by the Line
> of Communication to the other End of the Gallery, and
> returned back again to the Ivory Ball, which attracted the
> Leaf-Brass, and suspended it as before. The whole length
> of the Line was 147 Feet. (Gray 1731a, 27)

In this context, the theories of effluvia that had been influential for centuries are at their limits, since they can no longer explain these occurrences. Nothing can flow from a glass tube over several hundred feet without a connection.

The same experiment was continued in open air. Starting at Whel- er's estate, they built a conductor crossing silk threads stretched between two rods. On July 14, 1729, the length reached 666 feet. The return channel, which would allow one experimenter at the end of the "line of communication" to report what happened to his friend at the other end, consisted of the human voice. Wheler and Gray called the results of their tests back and forth to each other. The time delay of this return channel was insignificant: Gray would not have been able to be at both ends of the setup at the same time to confirm what happened or to determine its speed.

From a single source, Gray and Wheler created two, even three different conductors, which led off simultaneously in various directions. However, time eventually caught up with the two researchers:

> We began about Seven o'Clock, or some little Time after,
> but before Eight the Attraction ceased: But whether this
> was caused by the Dew falling, or by my being very hot,
> we could not positively say, but I rather impute it to the
> latter. (Gray 1731a, 31)

There are no reports of any continuation of these experiments. Instead, there was a shift from experimenting with lengths to surfaces: in what may be called an unintentional anticipation of the global village, Gray and Wheler electrified a twenty-seven-square-foot world map. They also found that a suspended circular wire would attract brass leaves located below it, provided that it was not too far away. While they were able to determine that the attraction worked to the same extent in all parts of the circular wire, they were not able to determine the location of electricity In the circle. What all these experiments have in common is that, no matter how long they attempted to make the connection, the effect was already there.

If electrifying objects requires the presence of the experimenter, who rubs the objects to achieve an effect, the transmitted effect must also happen in his absence—that means when there is no separation in the connection with the cable. Presence is no longer the condition of possibility for making both ends touch but rather the necessary result of the transmission. Because electricity is present at both ends at once, it is present everywhere. The cable has become not only a medium but, more specifically, a medium of immediacy—which is impossible in the framework of the physics of that time.

Bodies no longer merely receive electricity—they conduct it. In addition to corpuscles, these bodies can also be human bodies. In April 1740, Gray conducted a spectacular experiment that would fascinate audiences throughout Europe and would be demonstrated in numerous derivations in the form of an "electric kiss." In the experiment, Gray would suspend a schoolboy horizontally from the ceiling, put brass leaves on the floor under his hands and his hand, and then touch his feet with a charged tube. At the opposite end of the boy's body, the brass leaf would float up to his head. In the electric kiss variation, replacing the brass leaf with another human being would make the latter get hit with a discharging spark. Indeed, as Gray would find out, the schoolboy does not even necessarily need to be suspended from the ceiling; it sufficed

[Figure 1.2]. Gray's Transmissions. Source: Johann Gabriel Doppelmayr, *Neu-entdeckte Phaenomena von bewunderswürdigen Würckungen der Natur* (Nürnberg: Fleischmann, 1744), Table II.

to put him on a wax pedestal. As in the case of the silk threads, Gray was using the principle of insulation without knowing it. Even when two boys were put on wax pedestals and connected with a wire, they would each exert a force of attraction. The discharging spark eliminated distance, wiping out difference and stressing discontinuity. However, only contact electrifies: "I then bid one Boy put his Finger upon the other Boy's wrist, and then he immediately became electrical" (Gray 1731b, 402).

If human beings are able to conduct electricity, then the experimenter becomes part of the experiment. The presence of an experimenter's body can explain many failures of the performance of similar experiments, such as when experimenters would touch the electrified tubes with their hands and cause the electricity to get lost at these human outlets. The body no longer functions as an electric receiver, but as a conductor, and, with that, enters into a state of excitement.

Two different forms of transmissions come together in Gray's experimental setup. On the one hand, electricity acts as a mediator, without any apparent medium, between one object and another, whenever these are approached or touched. On the other hand, electricity gets transmitted to a distant place, making other objects become electric and, with that, conductors, transforming the wire into a cable. This distance opens a space. In passing something on from one object to another, a "line of communication" communicates, as in another meaning of this concept, designating military supply lines. But the instances of transmission in this "line of communication" are tripled: from one object to another at the starting point; through an object in the middle; from this object to another at the other end. The middle term can be extended to almost any desired length.

In London during the winter of the year following his first experiments, Gray would continue his research in this direction, finding out that the objects "communicating" with each other did not need to be connected to each other directly. There was an effect even at a little distance: no contact was necessary. It was sufficient to bring an electrified tube in the proximity of a conductor: "communication" would succeed even without contact. As Gray realized, the conductor would even attract a brass leaf at a distance:

> By these Experiments we find that the Electrick Vertue
> may not only be carried from the Tube by a Rod or a
> Line to distant Bodies, but that the same Rod or Line will
> communicate that Vertue to another Rod or Line that is
> at a Distance from it, and by that another Rod or Line the
> Attractive Force may be carried to other distant Bodies.
> (Gray 1731b, 404)

It is not necessary for the conductor to "immediately touch" the body at the end, for the ball to transmit immediately, as the French physicist Charles de Cisternay Dufay would report about the same experiment (Dufay 1733).

Hence, Gray's work marks two shifts in electricity research: first, it demonstrates that certain materials are able to transport the force of attraction over long distances when they are insulated; second, it shows that a conducting third can be switched in between two objects. These two shifts allow Gray to create effects that have never existed before. The communicability of electricity constitutes a new challenge because it detaches the object of research from cosmology and theories of substances (see Ben-Chaim 1990).

Nonetheless, this communicability of electric effects does not exhaust itself in research on physical conductivity. The early history of electric transmission cannot be described solely in terms of the history of physics. It depends equally on the stubborn materiality of the cable. The wire leads an experimental life of its own. As a medium, it is open to diverse ways of being used—above all, as a medial binder. It intervenes in experiments because it breaks, is resistant, or leaks energy. A wire can be bent into spirals and circles, squares and cubes. It opens up spaces and times, makes connections possible, and allows for connections to disappear immediately (on the history of wires, see Blake-Coleman 1992).

The Material Space of Distance

In his theory of the parasite as the "third" participating in every relation, Michel Serres attempts to grasp the place of difference, which is also the place of the cable: "A third exists before the second. A third exists before the other. [. . .] There is always a mediate, a middle, an intermediary" (Serres 1982, 63). As soon as the "line of communication" gets extended to the point that Gray can no longer hold it in his hands, the constellation changes. The channel creates a medial, material connection between two bodies, and constitutes a necessary technical condition of telecommunication. Although the effect apparently proceeds through a medium, instantaneity seems to negate this medium, since the simultaneity of cause and effect seemingly extends beyond any speed. With Gray, the fascination with simultaneity has materialized in an experimental setup for the first time. The same fascination will follow physics up to the present.[4]

There is a medium, but there is no delay in mediation. Gray makes out "no perceivable difference" in the effects of his experiment (Gray 1731a). An electrified body is seemingly "immediately" electric

(Hauksbee 1719/2004, 141; Dufay 1733, 259; Watson 1746, 727; Wheler 1739, 100)—immediately in all its parts, without any time delay or transmission time. What Gray terms a "difference" in the above statement is twofold: the repetition of an attraction that stays the same over the course of multiple tests and a temporal delay that he is unable to recognize as such. Nothing disturbs or inhibits the immediate simultaneity of transmission—and yet, the difference between the two places in the garden still represents a spatial division between them.

This relation of separation and connection is reflected in the dichotomous status of the cable: it is present in both places, but only because the other end is absent in that place. This is how the cable is able to carry proximity to a distance, and play out its function as a medium: it repeats and delays an electric effect. In this sense, transmission determines a difference because it makes a difference: the cable creates a spatial difference in terms of the cable's ends. According to the rules of Aristotelian and Newtonian physics, any spatial distance requires time to be overcome, if speed is not to be instantaneous. However, the force overcoming space here was electricity, and nobody knew whether it required time (see Marvin 1988). Everything was pointing in the direction that it did not. Since transmission time lies below every sensory threshold, it could be eliminated without any remainder. For Gray, electric transmission appears to be timeless. The events occurring at the ends of the cable do not run in parallel; they are connected through a material medium, and not merely an effluvial or an etherial one. In turn, immediacy is projected onto this medium, which also serves to negotiate the new status of absence and presence. This physics of electricity, evident in the case of the cable, shakes the foundations of science because in its theoretical framework, instantaneous action at a distance is impossible. For this reason, writing the history of the cable and its transmissions requires casting a glance at the transformations of physical knowledge at the time of Gray's experiments. They are also the setup in which the term "medium" is shaped in the form that became predominant throughout the twentieth century.

Although many ideas about the utopia of transmitting messages
at a distance were in circulation at the time, Gray's experiments
did not link up with them. "Communication," in the sense of the
physical sciences, cannot simply be equated with "communication" between people, though their conceptual histories are
intertwined. Gray's transmission is not a precursor of telegraphy,
despite having an identical experimental system. Its content is
itself—transmissibility. In Gray's experiments, there is no function
or processing, either in the mathematical sense or in the sense
of an application, and thus nothing is transmitted other than the
transmissibility of electrical attraction. The transmission is not
processed, and yet it shows, through attraction, that it exists. There
is no content of this communication, which is why it refers to itself
and thus exposes its properties. Transmission here means that the
same action happens in the same moment at the beginning and at
the end. It appears to be instantaneous, without time loss or delay.
If there is no transmission speed and thus no separation despite
distance, the two bodies involved in the communication are united
in their electricity. In this way, electricity is able not only to arrive,
"live," at the other end but also to be present at both places.

Only decades later, transmission time, as transport time or signal
time, will itself become a topic of inquiry only after there are more
precise measuring procedures for displaying speeds and delays.
Eventually, it will turn out that every cable influences what it transmits, and that resistance is a variable of transmission. Without this
knowledge, long-distance transmission is impossible. At the time of
Gray's experiments, there was no way to perceive the disturbances
and temporal delays of electricity, which will become functions of
cables—for example, in the laying of the transatlantic cable—since
these functions are dependent on measuring devices that divide
time or space and make it countable. The sole basis for Gray's judgment, defining the region in which something can be determined
to be "present," was sensory perception. At best, Gray and Wheler
were able to shout when something happened. But as soon as they
would raise their voices, it had already happened. Additionally, the
experimental setups were too large for perception. As long as no

measuring instruments were available, electric transmission could only be described as instantaneous: it was not possible to study its speed by the means of perception. In the end, the return channel would need to transmit just as fast as the electrical conductor (see Galison 2003). This is true even if the conductor is laid in a circle, thereby bringing both ends together into a single point that can be observed at once. The main aspiration running through all the work in physics on electrical action at a distance is to determine and to measure this time as a physical time, an objective time, a time beyond the experimenter's limited capacities of perception—and as a time of the cable.

As the wire becomes a cable, there are several noteworthy changes: a new time-dimension of transmission appears, and, with that, the possibility of storage. The electric cable transmits only attraction, without storage and without processing. Today, every signal that gets transmitted has to be processed in order to achieve "liveness" and "real-time" (e.g., in digital television transmissions). Even though processing time increasingly approaches transmission time, the term "real-time" remains a euphemism, and the rhetoric of "telepresence" skips over the production of that presence (see Sprenger 2015). There is transmission in "real-time." Every transmission is always mediated, and it is this delay that all technical media operate with. Real-time can only mean that signals are arriving at the speed in which they can be processed as quickly as possible: in time rather than real-time. Real-time always takes place between two points in time and is therefore not instantaneous. Skipping over this delay means ignoring its influence on how we are connected and disconnected.

Allowing the cable to come undone in processes of "instantaneity" and "acceleration" amounts to concealing the spatial relations, the spaces and times of interruption that are created by electric media. It also amounts to obscuring how these media are currently reconfiguring society. However, it is still important to keep in mind the deployment of the cable in the imaginary of its time. In the earliest discourses of telegraphy, there was a hope that the establishment of a telegraph line would do away with distances around the world, ultimately bringing people, countries, and continents closer together (for example Winkler 1750, 5). In this way, telegraphy catalyzes both new ideas about community and for communities' self-perception. As one developer of the telegraph, Carl August von Steinheil, put it:

> Communication is the strongest bond of the living creation: it connects one individual life to another, reproduces in one that which is a given for all, and thus forms out of individual beings species that emerge again as organic beings. (Steinheil 1838, 3)

The centrality of the cable for this imagination of an organic bond can be seen in an illustration of a figure, alluding to Shakespeare's Puck, alias Robin Goodfellow, who holds both ends of a cable wrapped around the globe: whenever he pulls one end, the other

" I'll put a girdle round about the earth in forty minutes."– SHAKSPEARE.

[Figure 1.3]. Historical Sketch of the Electric Telegraph. Source: Alexander Jones, *Historical Sketch of the Electric Telegraph* (New York: Putnam, 1852), frontispiece.

moves. In this case, the cable is a transmitter and a receiver at the same time and, as such, does not merely connect individual places to each other but rather forms a connection that ends where it began—exactly in the sense of a line in Shakespeare's *Midsummer Night's Dream:* "I'll put a girdle round about the earth in forty minutes." The illustration comes from Alexander Jones's *Historical Sketch of the Electric Telegraph,* which appeared in 1852, before the first attempt to lay a transatlantic cable but already anticipating a wired world.

Until it became measurable a century later with elaborate devices and experimental setups, electricity appeared not to have any propagation speed but rather seemed to be at different places at the same time. In this instantaneity, electricity is related to media concepts used in the twentieth century to narrate the history of this very medium. "Past, present, and future merge into electric nowness," Marshall McLuhan will write more than two hundred years after Gray's experiments (McLuhan and Nevitt 1973, 1). For McLuhan, the instantaneous, simultaneous transmission of the "electric age" will unite the world into a new entity without an outside. For Gray, too, instantaneity no longer refers only to a constellation present before one's eyes that can be perceived with a single glance, but to the expansion of a transmission in a space no longer based on the senses. In these phantasms of immediacy, the channel recedes from the picture because the instantaneity of ubiquity creates a new entity out of individuals, as in McLuhan's global village, in which the delays and the materialities of the cable are entirely eliminated.[5]

Territories of the Cable

The geographic space of transmission, the distance from one side of a garden to the other, is not identical with the territory produced by the cable. Whereas this territory depends on the smallest possible times, or even no time at all, the geographic space of transmission remains as it is. Without electric transmission, a cable

is merely a piece of wire, which nevertheless opens up a space. But
once this space can be crossed instantaneously, or almost instantaneously, it ceases to be an obstacle and—simplifying things, since
new problems and possibilities arise—must be conceived of anew.
The separation between transmitter and receiver, between glass
tube and brass leaf, ceases to be of minor importance, because
the medium between them has been invisibly extended—and
above all, because the length of the cable seems to be irrelevant
for transmission time.[6] The spatialization of the channel plays no
role for time: regardless of how long a cable may be, its end will
always already be at the beginning. Opening up a territory by laying
a cable creates new spaces and temporal relations. They define a
space of address.

Materially, the two communicants are relegated to a position
at each end of the cable, a position that, in transmitting from a
distance, becomes a location within a new spatial structure that
is not based on perception. This location can be addressed in
both orders—in the geographic order as in the territorial order of
the cable. In each order, however, the cable enters into different
relations, and borders different places. While closing off geography,
transmission also opens up a new space in which one end of a
garden is made to border the other, insofar as both are addresses,
just as Washington will later border Baltimore, or Britain will border
America, with the construction of the first telegraph lines. Even if
transmission is supposed to be instantaneous, its materiality opens
new spatial relations that start to change the world.

If the space and time of transmission are not conceived of as immediate, the duration of transmission necessarily requires space,
and the distance of transmission necessarily requires time. Both
are based on a delay that contradicts their presence. Conceiving
of the cable in terms of immediacy makes its in-betweenness disappear, and, with that, space and time of media as well. However,
the difference between the beginning and the end of a cable,
qua *différance,* transforms the phantasmal unity of transmitted
electricity into a duality. Communication inserts an interval into the

unity, an interval that is, to take up a thought of Jacques Derrida, equally different:

> This *différance* of the *between,* this elementary *différance* of inter-position or intervals between two surfaces is at the same time the condition of contact and the originarily spaced opening that calls for technical prosthetics and makes it possible, without any delay. (Derrida 2007, 229–30)

In other words, distinguishing A from B requires determining A by determining B, and this implies a delay: temporally, A comes before B, and between them comes the cable. As a spatialization of transmission, the cable causes delays due to the fact that both ends of the cable are predetermined to be addresses of transmission. This is due to the differentiating function of space: wherever A is located, B cannot be located, and, for this reason, there has to be a distance between them, which also differentiates them from each other. In terms of time, however, B can also be A'. The phantasmal immediacy of action at a distance, in which an action can be present at two or more places at the same time, would eliminate all of this: it would make A out of B, thereby wiping out division and disconnection. Ironically, the Leipzig-based cable researcher Johann Heinrich Winkler, who continued Gray's experiments a few years later, remarked as early as 1750: "At present, the speed of communicated [or, transmitted] electricity cannot be determined due to a lack of the required space" (Winkler 1750).

Thus, the cable is a measuring tape, a stopwatch, and a carrier rolled into one. It serves not only to transmit information or energy, but also to measure these transmissions in terms of their extent, speed, and distance, and to enable research on the space of transfer. In doing so, however, the cable intervenes in the transmission, since the speed of electric transmission, as would later become evident, is relative to cable length. In this sense, the cable requires research about the places where it is laid, such as knowledge about the peaks and valleys it has to cross, or the depth of the sea it gets lowered into. The cable and its long enigmatic resistance have ensured that the effect at its end is not identical with that at its beginning; even with the best insulation, there will inevitably be a loss. At first, this was not measurable because there were no corresponding instruments and dimensions, no units transforming space and time into measurable amounts. The history of the cable as a medium between immediacy and mediation is related to a history of measuring and proportioning electricity.

After Gray, the subsequent course of electricity research would be inconceivable without the cable. What would become known as the first stable functioning electromagnetic telegraph, created by Carl Friedrich Gauß and Wilhelm Weber in Göttingen in 1833, was initially nothing other than an experimental cable system, which served their research on the galvanic chain and their attempt to validate Ohm's law. With Georg Simon Ohm, the cable appears as a medium of delay and shows a resistant materiality. Ohm would formalize the principle of electrical resistance, which, in turn, is the foundation for the worldwide rise of telegraphy. The second half of the nineteenth century will become the age of long-distance cables, not only for the purposes of transmitting information but also, starting in the mid-1880s, for transferring energy. Thanks to the telegraph network, built to a global scale, the cable will become a medium of universality. Above all, cable research will come into its own, with the laying of the undersea cables, as a unique scientific field with protagonists like William Thomson and Michael Faraday whose starting point will be disturbances of communication and not its success (see Volmar 2009).

In short, since Gray's experiments, the cable temporalizes spatialization, it overcomes space in time, thereby creating a time between two places. The cable requires, systematically and physically, a rudimentary storage function: the contents of any transmission that is not instantaneous have to be stored, at least temporarily, because they have to exist somewhere, in some state, during the duration of the transmission. Electricity and cables, and later on, signals and messages, exist only in their execution, in performance, in circulation. And electricity can be measured only in this execution. At the end of every cable, the same effect that entered into it at the beginning should ultimately arrive. In Gray's experiments with the cable, this repetition consists solely of the effect of attraction. However, with the development of better measuring instruments, more reliable sources of electricity, and, above all, the breakthrough of electromagnetism, this repetition will have become standardized only several decades later to the point that the cable can be equipped with signals, eventually making it the basis for telegraphy and finally the transmission of the binary signals that still constitute our digital cultures. Transmission relocates effects to the places determined by a wire, which, for this very reason, has already become a cable.

Notes

1   While the history of the transatlantic cable is well known and Nicole Starosielskis media ethnography has explored submarine cables in detail, the histories and uses of shorter cables, for example in the domestic context, remains opaque.

2   For a deconstruction of communication as a separation that presupposes a connection, see Chang 1996.

3   Eustachius a Sancto Paulo, *Summa Philosophiae* (1614), qtd. in Spitzer 1948, 201.

4   For more detail, see Sprenger 2012.

5   For a recent iteration of these phantasms, see (Isenstadt 2018, 14–16). For Isenstadt, instantaneity, immediacy, and action at a distance are simply given physical and technical phenomena, which is wrong: no physicist of that time would have agreed that electricity is instantaneous or that action at a distance is possible. Newton, Faraday, and Maxwell, whom Isenstadt quotes, explicitly rejected this perspective. The seeming instantaneity of all-at-onceness that was established with telegraphy nonetheless became a cultural phantasm that Isenstadt's book on lighting explores in great detail, while still adhering to the phantasmatic dimension of immediacy.

6   For experiments following up on Gray's experiments, see Desaguliers (1734).

References

Aristotle. 2008. *Physics.* Oxford: Oxford University Press.

Ben-Chaim, Michael. 1990. "Social Mobility and Scientific Change: Stephen Gray's Con-

tribution to Electrical Research." *British Journal for the History of Science* 22, **27**
no. 22: 3–24.

Blake-Coleman, B. C. 1992. *Copper Wire and Electrical Conductors: The Shaping of a Technology*. Chur: Harwood.

Cantor, G. N. 1981. "The Theological Significance of Ethers." In *Conceptions of Ether: Studies in the History of Ether Theories 1740–1900*. Edited by G. N. Cantor and M. J. S. Hodge, 135–56. Cambridge: Cambridge University Press.

Chang, Briankle. 1996. *Deconstructing Communication*. Minneapolis: University of Minnesota Press.

Chipman, R.A. 1954. "An Unpublished Letter of Stephen Gray on Electrical Experiments, 1707–1708." *Isis* 45, no. 1: 33–40.

Derrida, Jacques. 2007. *On Touching—Jean-Luc Nancy*. Stanford, Calif.: Stanford University Press.

Desaguliers, John. 1734. *A Course of Experimental Philosophy: Volume I*. London: W. Innys and T. Longman.

Dufay, Charles. 1733. "A Letter from Mons. Du Fay, F. R. S. and of the Royal Academy of Sciences at Paris to His Grace Charles Duke of Richmond and Lenox Concerning Electricity." *Philosophical Transactions* 38:258–66.

Galison, Peter. 2003. *Einstein's Clocks, Poincaré's Maps: Empires of Time*. New York: Norton.

Gray, Stephen. 1720. "An Account of Some New Electrical Experiment." *Philosophical Transactions* 31:104–7.

Gray, Stephen. 1731a. "A Letter to Cromwell Mortimer, M. D. Secr. R. S. Containing Several Experiments Concerning Electricity." *Philosophical Transactions* 37:18–44.

Gray, Stephen. 1731b. "Two Letters from Mr. Stephen Gray, F.R.S. to C. Mortimer, M.D. Secr. R. S. Containing Farther Accounts of His Experiments Concerning Electricity." *Philosophical Transactions* 37:397–407.

Hauksbee, Francis. 1719/2004. *Physico-Mechanical Experiments: Reprint*. With the assistance of John Henry. Bristol: Thoemmes Continuum.

Heilbron, John L. 1979. *Electricity in the 17th and 18th Centuries: A Study in Early Modern Physics*. Berkeley: University of California Press.

Hesse, Mary B. 1955. "Action at a Distance in Classical Physics." *Isis* 46, no. 4: 337–53.

Hunt, Bruce. 1994. "The Ohm Is Where the Art Is: British Telegraph Engineers and the Development of Electrical Standards." *Osiris* 9, no. 9: 48–63.

Isenstadt, Sandy. 2018. *Electric Light: An Architectural History*. Cambridge, Mass.: MIT Press.

Marvin, Carolyn. 1988. *When Old Technologies Were New: Thinking about Communications in the Late Nineteenth Century*. Oxford: Oxford University Press.

McLuhan, Marshall, and Barrington Nevitt. 1973. "The Argument: Causality in the Electric World." *Technology and Culture* 14, no. 1: 1–18.

Peters, John D. 2000. *Speaking into the Air: A History of the Idea of Communication*. Chicago: University of Chicago Press.

Peters, John D. 2006. "Technology and Ideology: The Case of the Telegraph Revisited." In *Thinking with James Carey. Essays on Communications, Transportation, History*, ed. Jeremy Packer and Craig Robertson, 137–56. New York: Peter Lang.

28 Schaffer, Simon. 1997. "Experimenters' Techniques, Dyers' Hands, and the Electric Planetarium." *Isis* 88, no. 3: 456–83.

Serres, Michel. 1982. *The Parasite.* Minneapolis: University of Minnesota Press.

Siegert, Bernhard. 1999. *Relays. Literature as an Epoch of the Postal System.* Stanford, Calif.: Stanford University Press.

Spitzer, Leo. 1948. "Milieu and Ambiance," in *Essays in Historical Semantics,* 179–225. New York: Vanni.

Sprenger, Florian. 2012. *Medien des Immediaten. Elektrizität, Telegraphie, McLuhan.* Berlin: Kadmos.

Sprenger, Florian. 2015. *Politics of Microdecisions: Edward Snowden, Net Neutrality, and the Architecture of the Internet.* Lüneburg: Meson Press.

Starosielski, Nicole. 2015. *The Undersea Network.* Durham, N.C.: Duke University Press.

Steinheil, Carl A. von. 1838. *Ueber Telegraphie, insbesonders durch galvanische Kräfte.* München: Wolf.

Volmar, Axel, ed. 2009. *Zeitkritische Medien.* Berlin: Kadmos.

Watson, William. 1746. "A Continuation of a Paper Concerning Electricity." *Philosophical Transactions* 44:695–749.

Wheler, Granvile. 1739. "Some Electrical Experiments, Chiefly Regarding the Repulsive Force of Electrical Bodies." *Philosophical Transactions* 41:98–125.

Winkler, Johann H. 1750. *Grundriss zu einer ausführlichen Abhandlung von der Electricität.* Leipzig: Breitkopf.

[2]

A Cornucopia of Meanwhiles

John Durham Peters

Oblivious Simultaneity

Events have always been happening at the same time. Billions of things are happening this very second around the globe, in my immediate vicinity, and even within my own body, all without my knowing anything about them. If it is overwhelming to think that about six thousand people die and fifteen thousand more are born every hour, abandon all hope of trying to track the mitosis of cells or the work of chlorophyll! Counting would fail if we tried to quantify all the things that happen without notice, especially once we dive into microscales! (Surely the number of unnoticed things vastly outstrips the number of things known or observed.) Oblivious simultaneity, as we might call it, seems simply part of the order of things. Our bits of awareness are rare and scattered lights on a dark landscape of unknowing. So the poets and philosophers have long told us. Everything flows, said Heraclitus; "Mudam-se os tempos," wrote Camões; "Nobody knows nothing anymore," sings Billy Bragg.

Conscious or controlling simultaneity, however, is quite a different animal. To know, narrate, or act upon another event occurring at the same time but in a different space requires a logistical link of some kind in matter or mind, in transportation or communication.

This essay explores human-based simultaneous action at a distance. It compiles a comparative history of meanwhile structures, which I define as techniques of shuttling between two points in space at the same time that are too far apart for the unaided human senses. From a patchwork of examples, several of them from that library of ancient literature gathered in the Bible, I hope a central point becomes clear: that banking time is a way to span space.

Anderson: Meanwhile Structures in Modernity—and Antiquity?

Benedict Anderson, in his highly influential *Imagined Communities: Reflections on the Origin and Spread of Nationalism* (1983), speculates that "every essential modern conception is based on a conception of 'meanwhile'" (24). He locates this particularly in the modern media ("forms of imagining") of the novel and the newspaper, and in his second edition of the book (1991), in the census, map, and museum as well. The novel "is a device for the presentation of simultaneity in 'homogeneous and empty time,' or a complex gloss upon the word 'meanwhile'" (25). A novel can jump horizontally between scenes—same time, different space—and tell of characters whose lives run in parallel and could cross unwittingly in the street without being aware of their remote links. "In *Imagined Communities*," he later wrote, "I argued that the historical appearance of the novel-as-popular-commodity and the rise of nation-ness were intimately related. Both nation and novel were spawned by the simultaneity made possible by clock-derived, man-made 'homogeneous empty time,' and thereafter, of Society understood as a bounded intrahistorical entity" (Anderson 1998, 334). (By *intrahistorical*, Anderson means secular or common time, not eternity; see Culler 1999.)

Anderson spins the story elegantly: once upon a time, history and cosmology were inseparable, and time present contained time past and time future. Now we live in a dull and disenchanted world, where the clock ticks away relentlessly and time flows in a straight line. (Hence the rise of nationalism as an answer to the question of meaning for men and women stripped of ancient religious frameworks.) This tale of a massive shift from sacred to secular, vertical to horizontal, recursive to linear time might be the founding story of modernity. "Our own conception of simultaneity," he states, "has been a long time in the making, and its emergence is certainly connected, in ways that have yet to be well studied, with the development of the secular sciences" (24). Antique narratives were not capable of cross-cutting, as the film-editing technique is called that takes you instantly from one scene to another—near or far—in a parallel time. Petronius's *Satyricon,* the scurrilous Roman novel, in some ways is a forerunner of the modern novel, but "its narrative proceeds single file" (25). There is no "in the meantime" movement from one scene to another.

Anderson places the big shift in the eighteenth century. Evidently borrowing from Marshall McLuhan, Anderson treats the essence of the newspaper as "calendrical coincidence" (33).[1] What all the news stories in a daily edition had in common was that they occurred yesterday. (The more recent 24/7 news cycle changes this circadian rhythm.) Readers of newspapers partake of "the diurnal regularities of the imagining life" (35n63): in both narrative structure (many events, one text) and audience behavior (many readers, one time) newspapers follow a logic of composite juxtaposition. In the middle ages, artists could portray local patrons at the birth of Jesus in Bethlehem without worrying about anachronism; now was then and here was there. Under the regime of modern clock time, in contrast, modern novelists and journalists learned to array events as parallel in space rather than time. At least so goes the argument.

Was Anderson right? Could events happening over great distances be coordinated when messages traveled no faster than foot, horse, pigeon, or ship? Were there no robust meanwhile structures before the eighteenth century? Did the apparently instantaneous transmissions of the telegraph enable new modes?

Biblical Fathers and Sons: Characters Transport Narrative Focus

Let's test Anderson's thesis with two of the Bible's most memorable narratives, both of which concern fathers and brothers separated in different places with very different fates. Neither story has any simultaneous back-and-forth between parallel developments until the brothers actually come back into the same place, bringing their time streams with them. In the book of Genesis, Joseph is sold into Egypt by his jealous brothers, who assume that he vanishes into servile anonymity. When a terrible famine later drives them into Egypt in search of food, they meet an imposing Pharaonic figure whom they don't realize is Joseph, who has—in the meanwhile— risen to the heights of the Egyptian world. The narration follows the physical movement of the brothers; it has no wings to jump from Egypt to Palestine. Likewise in the parable of the father and two sons told in the book of Luke, the younger, "prodigal" son demands his inheritance, moves to a far country, and squanders his wad in what the King James Version memorably calls "riotous living." When he returns in frustrated impoverishment, his father welcomes him home royally, much to the umbrage of the older, faithful brother. We never hear of the two brothers at the same time in different places; the two narrative streams only come together when the brothers do. What is interesting here is not the parallel development of separate stories. That has always happened. What is interesting is the lack of narrative means for saying "meanwhile, back at the ranch." The narrative proceeds, as Anderson says, single file; it does not outpace the physical limits of the characters' movements. There is no magic carpet that carries the reader telegraphically to different places. The moment of recognition is only possible with physical presence.

Prophetic Vision: Live Feed or Memory?

Yet in both the Bible and in Homer, there is such a magic carpet device—but apparently only for the gifted and for gods. The book of Ezekiel gives us the first. The first verse sets up the drama: the heavens open up to a visionary man located in unusually specific circumstances: by the Kebar river, in Babylon (Iraq), among a group of captives, on the fifth day of the fourth month of the thirtieth year. The Jews are in Babylonian captivity, far away from home. But Ezekiel, with its colorful and weird imagery as well extreme behavior by the narrator, is a psychedelic, literally trippy book, especially with the narrator's frequent flights between Babylon and Jerusalem. The spirit moves him, levitating or teleporting him through the air, where he witnesses people and buildings, especially the temple in Jerusalem, from his location in Iraq. It is not clear whether he is supposed to be accessing events archived in memory or viewing a live feed. When Ezekiel sees, for example, a prince of the people named Pelatiah die in Jerusalem (Ez. 11:13), is this supernaturally privileged access to news he could not have received so quickly in Babylon by normal means or a recounting of an already known event? No one could know without a system of verification that at that time would have to travel on land.

The Homeric Meanwhile?

In Homer, the gods of course are not bound to the sluggish speeds of earth travel. Athena can zoom from the Phaeacians to Olympus and back where she appears to the shipwrecked Odysseus in veiled form (*Odyssey,* book 6); she serves as the puppet master of the several plots in the *Odyssey,* tracking down Telemachus, the long-missed son of Odysseus, in Sparta, for instance, at the opening of book 15 before she jets back to Olympus. Telemachus then approaches Ithaca in his ship while Odysseus feasts and tells identity-cloaking war stories with his friend Eumaeus the swineherd. At line 301 the narrative wings from Telemachus steering his way through the rocky islands around the island to the hut where Odysseus, Eumaeus, and others are hanging out. The transition is marked by a well-known Homeric formula that means something like "but then, on the other hand," but doesn't commit us to understanding it as a "meanwhile," though it is sometimes translated that way.[2]

There is no single point of view on the island that I know of where a physical viewer could have stood to take in both the hut and the ship synoptically. In a similar way, book 16 of the *Odyssey* shifts focus between the palace, the hut, and the ship on the shore. The narrative slices through space with the same speed that Athena flies.

As these examples suggest, narrative structure with regard to space and time in Homer is highly varied and complex. There is a more than century-old debate in Homer studies about Zielinski's law, which decrees that simultaneous events in Homer are always narrated as sequential. Early on, the debate was inspired by the Anderson-like and perhaps condescending thought that ancient authors could not imagine simultaneous events, but the obvious point that Homer is a poet of enormous narrative prowess who handles time and space in a variety of ways, not always consistent, has been made by many scholars since. (For an excellent overview see Scodel 2008). But for us the relevant point is that brilliant scholars have not been able to settle the question for good whether there are meanwhile structures in Homer. That the question is open is itself a sign that his narrative world was different than that of the modern newspaper or novel, where there could be no such question. Anderson both offers too stark a historical narrative of before-and-after *and* sees something important about modern narrative organization.

Eratosthenes: A Priori Synchronization

Eratosthenes, the third-century BCE Greek mathematician, astronomer, and chief librarian of Alexandria, was the first that we know of to arrive at an accurate estimate of the earth's size. He did so via a thought-experiment that put two distant places into one time. There are learned debates about his methods—did he take shadows from wells, towers, or sundials? What are the modern equivalents of his measurements? Did he round his calculations for arithmetic convenience? But here is one account of what he did: He knew that on the summer solstice that the sundial in Alexandria, in northern Egypt, showed a shadow of 7.2 degrees. He also knew that at Aswan, 5000 stadia to the south on the same meridian, there was no shadow at noon on the same date: the sunlight went straight down to the bottom of a well. He assumed a round earth, and perfectly parallel rays of sunlight. He didn't need a telegraph relay from Aswan to tell him that the sun was casting no shadow at noon; he knew that already and took it as given. The regularity of planetary rotation obviated the need for fresh data. Astronomical constants do not require empirical confirmation and remain invariant compared to noisier and more mutable kinds of data, such as weather data. Using basic *geometry*—quite literally, the science of earth measurement—he inferred that the angle of the shadow at Alexandria would be the same as the angle from the center of the earth to the two cities (see Figure 1). This angle was 7.2 degrees, or one fiftieth of a circle (7.2/360 = 1/50), so Eratosthenes figured that the distance from Aswan to Alexandria, known to

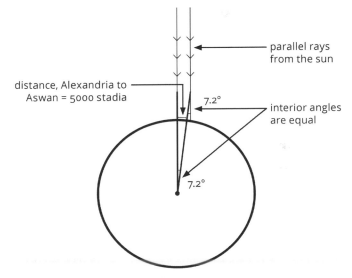

[Figure 2.1]. Inspired by Ryan (2016: 372).

be 5000 stades, was one fiftieth of the circumference of the earth. 5000 x 50 = 250,000 stades. If, as one historian concludes, a stade was about 157.7 meters, then Eratosthenes's estimate was 39,425 kilometers, which is remarkably close to the earth's equatorial circumference of 40,075 km (Engels 1985). (The earth, like many of us, bulges at the middle, and its meridional or north–south circumference is 40,008 km.)

The Hare and the Hedgehog

Eratosthenes engaged in what we can call space-axis manipulation, a term I owe to Paul Frosh. This is an odd and interesting kind of action at a distance. In such a priori synchronization, a single person combines two observations in the nonlinear time of memory to fly across one fiftieth of the earth's surface. But let us be more precise. Eratosthenes did not have to fly across the two spaces. He was already in both, or at least had instantaneous knowledge of conditions of both spots at once. He operated in the symbolic realm free of the grind of real time. His memory was a random-access database. This is timeless simultaneity, as explicated by Hartmut Winkler in a brilliant essay (Winkler 2009 and 2015, 233–54). Building on the Grimm Brothers tale of a race between a hare and a hedgehog in which the hedgehog, obviously a much slower runner, always wins, Winkler contrasts two modes of operating in space and time. The hare always uses up time in running the race, however little. The hedgehog, however, requires no time to traverse point A and point B because he—or she—is already there. That is, the hedgehog cheats by stationing at the endpoint of the track his wife, whom the hare mistakes for the original hedgehog. Whichever direction the hare runs, he finds the hedgehog already there, victorious. The hare can never win against an opponent who spans space instantaneously. The hare must always pay a toll to time. Because the hedgehog has taken advantage of earlier time to pre-distribute over space, travel is free. Or rather, no travel is necessary. In memory, like any archival system that gathers many moments into an instantaneous array, the past and the present are

contemporaneous. (This is the mode of apprehending time that
Anderson thought uniquely medieval or sacred; it is in fact one of
the fundamental modes of—nonlinear—temporal organization.)
The hare mode is typical of media operations that transmit, such as
telegraphy and telephony; the hedgehog mode is typical of media
operations that spread all at once in advance, such as publishing.
(We ignore the many further subtleties here.) Most narratives inch
along in hare mode. A play like *Hamlet* jumps between different
characters and scenes, but the implication is that we are in a weird
kind of diachrony. Eratosthenes, rather than rapid movement,
had a real simultaneity. So, with help of earth, sun, and memory,
meanwhile structures were possible, at least rarely, in the ancient
world.

The New Moon: Synchronization Plus Buffering

Contingent and variable data cannot be handled hedgehog style.
Such data perish in time, and so transit speed affects their value.
The moon's phases are an example. The ancient Jewish calendar
pivoted on the new moon, which marked the beginning of the
month and of many holidays.[3] The new moon must be sighted but
varies slightly by point of view on earth. A new moon occurs when
the moon is between the earth and the sun; it is therefore invisible
by the naked eye for a variable period of around twenty-four hours.
The paradoxical challenge is to spot something that you can't see,
so you settle for the first sliver of the crescent as proof of the new
moon. Determining when it is at its smallest (= newest) is always a
judgment call with potential for a slight geographic bias. Another
complexity was that the Jerusalem Sanhedrin held a monopoly on
determining the new moon until the fourth century, when Hillel II
introduced a regular calendar. To send the signal to a people scattered across the ancient Middle East faced many perils. Its drag left
ambiguity about its accuracy: the speed of transmission always affects time-sensitive information. The solution reached was to grant
double holidays to the diaspora: assuming that remote intelligence

might be unreliable, you build in a fudge-factor to account for message latency. (Even with instant signal transmission today, most of the diaspora observes double holidays; some pleasant things live on even after the reason for their origin has passed.) Delay was not the only problem: so were faulty or corrupt witnesses, tampering with the fire signals, clouds or fog that obscured sighting of the moon or the fire signal, slow messengers or ones who refused to travel on a holy day, etc. (If the announcement of the holiday causes its messengers to violate its sanctity by traveling on it, this is an odd contradiction. The fact of the holiday would be news that that fact makes unshareable!)[4] The strategy here is synchronization plus buffering to allow for lag times to pool and catch up or run ahead.

Information Is Never Free

It is dangerous to be a messenger. For a messenger bringing unwelcome news to a volatile tyrant, never was McLuhan's equation of medium and message more fraught. In the first chapter of 2 Samuel, an Amalekite soldier brings news to David of the death of his sometime opponent and father-in-law King Saul. David asks how he knows that Saul is genuinely dead. The messenger tells of coming upon Saul after his unsuccessful attempt to fall on his sword. The Amalekite finds Saul badly wounded but agonizingly still alive; Saul asks him to kill him, and he complies. In telling David this, the messenger thought he was currying favor; instead he was confessing to a crime. The admission cost him his life, as David orders his henchmen to murder him. This story leans toward a crucial quantum discovery: that information is never free. Information is ontologically part of the system: you cannot observe a system without engaging it. Maxwell's demon is the fantasy of costless information—a fantasy that went down, literally, in smoke. The universe will run down; information is intervention. These two truths have much to do with each other. The nature of the cosmos and the limits of our knowledge are one. And the nature of the cosmos is that time runs in only one direction: anything we know comes at the expense of time (Kittler 2003).

Dialectic of Buffering

A lot can happen while a message is buffering. The book of 1 Samuel tells the episode of the city of Jabesh threatened by the Ammonites. The elders of the city ask for seven days to send messengers throughout Israel to see if anyone of their compatriots will come to their aid. Officially they are asking for time to transmit a message, but they are also gaining time to mobilize. The transmission of the data is also the readying of an army. In such situations signal and ontology most closely approach each other. Much mischief can occur between point A and point B in hare mode. Aristotle, in the *Politics,* smirks that Babylon was more a nation than a city: "Babylon, they say, had been taken for three days before some part of the inhabitants became aware of that fact."[5] Aristotle thought it absurd that a polis would not be in instantaneous communication with itself. It was supposed to be a single body, "always already in synchrony" as Helge Jordheim remarks.[6]

But even bodies are not self-transparent. Herrmann von Helmholtz discovered the finite speed of nervous propagation in the 1840s, forever ending the fantasy of complete self-unity. "I think, therefore I am" was now "I think, therefore I am belated." Imagine the split second in which I have died but my brain hasn't gotten the news yet. Of course, the fact that I am alive enough not to know I am dead suggests I might not yet be dead. The body, like the ancient Jewish diaspora or a metropolis like Babylon, could never be on one precise same time grid. Where the ancient world could only imagine the terror of organic mismatch for the Leviathan of a state like Babylon, after Helmholtz it was a fact written into all nervous systems. That held especially for the Leviathans of *Moby-Dick,* whales whose long nerves suggested potentially significant syncing mismatches. Did their two, entirely independent, non-binocular eyes cause them to live in a synthetically integrated immersive now-time, or did they require a completely different mode of being in time (see *Moby-Dick,* chapter 74)? The problem of communication within the polis moved to the physical body.

The Moon: Romantic Simultaneity

Separated lovers have at least the moon in common. Probably every generation has rediscovered that the moon can serve as a transponder for bouncing heartthrobs to other parts of the earth. The moon as an instantaneous relay was expressed by the Tang poet Zhang Jiuling (678–740 CE) in "Looking at the Moon and Thinking of One Far Away" (望月怀远). In one translation (Bynner 1982, 66):

> The moon, grown full now over the sea,
> Brightening the whole of heaven,
> Brings to separated hearts
> The long thoughtfulness of night.
> It is no darker though I blow out my candle.
> It is no warmer though I put on my coat.
> So I leave my message with the moon
> And turn to my bed, hoping for dreams.

According to Su Hua, one of the lines may be translated more directly as "the sea gives birth to the moon (and) even the ends of the earth share the moment." She also points to the closing line of a famous poem by Su Shi (1037–1101 CE), the many-sided poet-statesman of the Song dynasty, called "Water Melody": "Though three hundred miles apart, we are still able to share the beauty of the moon together." That poem's "I" says he wishes to ride the wind but fears the cold of the high altitudes and settles instead on a reverie with the moon beams. In a different mode, Li Bai, perhaps China's most famous poet and, like Zhang from the Tang dynasty, tells of drinking alone to the moonlight, the moon and its shadow providing company for him and making three total. Here, of course, is no synchronization, only the moon as a companion for the lonely—as it was a go-between for the separated lovers in the other poets.[7] René Girard's point, made in a series of books starting in the early 1960s (see Girard, 1961) that romantic love always involves a third party, was never more true.

The Christian Gospels recount many episodes of Jesus healing people. Sometimes he touches them, or they touch him, and sometimes he concocts medicaments on the spot of mud and spittle. Yet he also often cures the sick at a distance, and in many instances touch is superfluous. For a comparative history of simultaneity, the most interesting episode (John 4:46–54) occurs when a royal official hears that Jesus has entered into Cana, a town in Galilee, and approaches him, asking him to come down to Capernaum, presumably a day's journey, in order to heal his son. Jesus says that he doesn't need to come and sends the man home, telling him that his son will be fine. The official trusts him and returns, and on the way is met by servants who tell him that his son has recovered. He asks them when it happened. The fever, they report, broke yesterday at the seventh hour (about one in the afternoon). Cross-checking the timestamp, the man realizes that was exactly when Jesus talked to him; he and his household become firm believers when they realize that the healing must have been caused by Jesus. The Gospel of John uses this retrospectively established simultaneity to make a point about the nature of faith, but it is a simultaneity discovered only after the fact by comparing two separate chronologies— standard for a world without any system of synchronizing time across distance.

The Genitive Absolute; Or, Event-Splices

If biblical narrative proceeds normally single file, there nevertheless are many examples of two things happening almost exactly at the same time. The four messengers to Job, announcing the four rapid disasters that destroy all his family and possessions, come in quick succession, each one overlapping slightly with the previous— following "hard upon," as *Hamlet* has it. There are two dramatic event splices, for instance, in Luke's story of the Passion. Luke 22:47 says that "while Jesus was yet speaking" the mob led by Judas came to arrest him. Peter then follows Jesus at a distance, warming himself at a fire and sputtering denials against curious onlookers who think they have seen him with Jesus. After the third denial, again "while he was yet speaking," the cock crows, Jesus turns and looks at him across the crowd, Peter remembers his promise never to deny and Jesus's warning that he would do so three times before the rooster sounded, and goes outside to weep bitterly. You can almost imagine the camerawork.

Erich Auerbach has wonderfully analyzed this episode already (see Auerbach 1946, chapter 2). I want to reflect more specifically on the ways the text treats time. This is not a modern meanwhile structure, because the figures remain within sensory range of each other; for me, a genuine meanwhile structure must involve cross-cutting between remote scenes. But the grammatical structure in Greek of the genitive absolute allows for the juxtaposition of two happenings, one suspended in the absolute, and the other with a finite verb. This kind of event-splice happens biblically when two happenings are within range of each other, not at a distance. The grammatical structure occurs hundreds of times in the New Testament, and more rarely in Homer, Thucidydes, and Plato (Fuller 2008). It links two happenings—causally, concessively, consecutively—by floating one in absolute form, and the other finite. Greek grammar enables meanwhile structures of a sort. But only if one is suspended in a tenseless (timeless) state.

Magic Carpet Rides

Almost as in Ezekiel, fast travel across great gulfs of space occurs in *The Book of a Thousand Nights and One Night*. In Richard Burton's translation: "Prince Husayn . . . spread his carpet upon the court-ground behind the Khan wherein he lodged, and sitting thereon, together with his suite and the steeds and all he had brought with him, mentally wished that he might be transported to the cara-vanserai where the three brothers had agreed to meet. No sooner had he formed the thought than straightway, in the twinkling of an eye, the carpet rose high in air and sped through space and carried them to the appointed stead where, still garbed as a merchant he remained in expectation of his brothers' coming."[8] The carpet is a hare, not a hedgehog, since it takes some time, even if only the twinkling of an eye, but the preestablished meeting point with his brothers suggests hedgehog-like preprocessing, the use of past time in order to set up a later cost-free simultaneity. You need to use expensive time to buy free time, or loose time to prepare for tight time. (Chess players know that bad moves lose tempo. A strong position is the same as having spare moves.)

Sympathetic Simultaneity

Francis Bacon explores eight forms of action at a distance: communicable diseases, light and sound, electricity and magnetism, gravity, interpersonal influences of affection and imagination, the influences of celestial bodies, sympathy, and "emission(s) of immateriate virtues" (Bacon 1844, 2:124). As is typical with Bacon, the list combines elements easily recognizable to us with ones that look weirdly medieval. Bacon clearly is a bit skeptical about the last one but feels called to investigate the idea "that in things, or the parts of things that have been once contiguous or entire, there should remain a transmission of virtue from the one to the other: as between the weapon and the wound" (126). He is referring to the practice of *unguentem teli,* or anointing at a distance, in which a salve applied to the sword that caused a wound will heal the wound, however far away its victim happens to be. It is a kind of hedgehog argument: an entire system retains its integral virtue, even when sundered. Bacon might have been interested to know of quantum entanglement, which is surely just as weird!

Longitude: Chronometer as Telegraph

Bernhard Siegert places the deep history of the modern quest for simultaneity at sea: in the problem of how to determine longitude (Siegert 2015). The rise of simultaneity to the forefront of early twentieth-century physics is not simply the culmination of a long history of scientific experimentation but also part of the history of an imperial struggle for power, for control over the seas, that goes back to the sixteenth century. Ptolemy, the late Greek astronomer and geographer, already designed a grid system of latitudes and longitudes, but it took on new life as a technology of power under the Portuguese and Spanish seaborne empires. Longitudes, of course, draw imaginary north–south lines from pole to pole. Because of the remarkably stable rotation of the earth's axis, north and south are essentially invariant within historical epochs, and latitude is relatively easy to calculate: a clear view of the horizon and a sighting of the North Star allows you find the angle between the two. That angle is your latitude. On the equator, the North Star is on the horizon, and your latitude is zero; at the North Pole, the North Star is directly overhead and your latitude is 90 degrees. (South of the equator you can use the Southern Cross instead of the North Star.) Finding your point on the east–west axis is, however, another matter. The earth is always spinning; there are no fixed celestial points to designate an invariant east or west. There could be no such thing as an East Star!

In 1530 the Belgian mathematician Gemma Frisius had the brilliant thought to use another point on earth as the standard for longitude. The earth rotates twenty-four hours a day, on annual average, and so a reliable clock on a sea voyage set to the local time of a distant place could indirectly indicate eastward or westward displacement from that longitude. Fifteen degrees of longitude equals one hour of the earth's rotation. The problem was that no clock could keep accurate enough time at sea to be functional, thanks to many factors including the rocking motion that threw off its spring balances and exposure to temperature, humidity, and water itself. For more than two centuries a reliable sea chronometer was a major agenda item for European science and technology, a problem in mechanics, metallurgy, and waterproofing, until the British clockmaker John Harrison decisively solved it in 1762. (The problem of longitude drove Christiaan Huyghens's invention of the second hand in 1657, among other innovations.) The notion of precision, which had long pertained only to the sky, was brought down to earth, or rather to sea. The exact measurements of celestial position that astronomers had been making since antiquity went horizontal. My eyes, my finger, that star; here at sea, clock, there at that time. If you know, for instance, that the sun rises at Greenwich at 4:42 a.m. on June 21, and you have a clock that gives you the exact time at Greenwich, and the sun rises for you when that clock says 8:42 a.m., and you are on the same latitude as Greenwich then you know that you are four hours later, i.e. 60 degrees west of Greenwich. (If you aren't on the same latitude, tables can help you make necessary adjustments.)

Here is something remarkable indeed: the complete fulfillment of the hedgehog principle. The ship and Greenwich are already in touch. Like Eratosthenes, there is no need to transmit any data. Both can count on the regularity of the earth and its rotation as a given. Such instantaneous communication might seem magical and silly in Bacon, but Greenwich and the ship do communicate in some odd way out of time. The clock serves as a wireless telegraph *avant la lettre,* a benign and portable doppelgänger of Greenwich. It receives intelligence from afar regardless of weather, pirates, interference, or glitches. Here is a time-and-space coordination system with little vulnerable infrastructure. A watch, said Norbert Wiener, is "a pocket orrery," or miniature model of the heavens. Heavenly patterns locate ships moving about the globe for economics and empire. Time here is a proxy for space.

Synkairization through Networks

What if we thought of syn-kair-ization as well as syn-chron-ization, if you will forgive the ugly term? That is exactly the crazy undertaking of meteorology, the gathering of many *kairoi* into one synoptic forecast. (*Kairos* means *weather* in modern Greek.) Meteorology is a privileged site for seeing changing conceptions of time, and modern weather data is perhaps the clearest of all domains for seeing space-time compression.

Local weather description existed from time immemorial, but in the 1780s came the first efforts to track large-scale weather events with real data. Natural philosophers had long sensed that local weather was dependent on remote conditions but because the speed of weather's change was greater than the speed of data's transit, same-day, large-scale weather events could only be studied and mapped after the fact. If it was hard to send data about the new moon in antiquity, it was even harder to send sufficient data about the fickle atmosphere. (Meteorology has always been a big-data science.) The very idea of a weather map was a major innovation—a map of quickly fluctuating things such as rainfall, temperature, or pressure instead of rivers, shorelines, and mountain ranges. In history maps were generally of constants, not variables. Indeed, until the late nineteenth century, climate science was a branch of geography until it was claimed by the physicists.[9]

German physicist F. W. Brandes may be the first to have made a weather map (1816). His plea for Europe-wide help on his project to reconstruct the weather in Europe of 1783 reveals the toil and trouble facing any ambitious weather knower before high-speed data transfer (Brandes 1819). His grand ambition was to map the temperature in Europe *"gleichzeitig"* or simultaneously. He complained how "utterly exhausting" it was to sort out a "host" (*Heer*) or "ocean" (*Meer*) of "a hundred thousand data-points" when only a few hundred belonged to each day (625). The glimpse of larger patterns gave some relief (*Aufmunterung*) from the toil. He was on the brink of discovering low-pressure cells, which far outspan the observable range of an individual tethered to the earth. (Only with space flight and satellites did global weather come into phenomenological range.) His textbook, *Beiträge zur Witterungskunde* (1820), also starts with weariness amid heaps of data. He had to sort through 180,000 discrete bits of data, 70,000 of which he gathered himself. The research process took him to the verge of total despair about "die so oft erfolglose Versuche etwas Regelmässiges in diesem Gewirre zu entdecken," the so often unsuccessful attempts to discover anything regular in this snarl; his

efforts were interrupted by the recurrent crushing (*niederschlagend*)
feeling of having accomplished nothing (iv). The subtitle announces
his more specific aim: "gleichzeitige Witterungs-Ereignisse in weit
von einander entfernten Weltgegenden." In 1820, the only way to
analyze "simultaneous weather-events in mutually remote regions
of the world" was retrospectively—and via networks. Weather
data had to be composite. A pressure system could be seen only
by many eyes and ears. For him, it took several decades to gather
enough data to map a single day's weather.

Timelines into Timepoints

William Charles Redfield (1798–1857), one of the first American
meteorologists, "didn't need an observer network, at least not at
first," says Mark Monmonier in his useful history of weather maps
(Monmonier 1999, 31). Traveling from western Massachusetts
to his home in Connecticut in 1821, Redfield noticed that trees
flattened in an earlier storm "were uniformly prostrated *towards
the south-east*" (21, original emphasis), while the trees that fell in
central Connecticut were all facing the northwest. Aha! He thought:
"*This storm was exhibited in the form of a great whirlwind*" (21, original)! A single person, endowed with a purse full of post-hoc flexible
time, could compile observations of a single event whose radius
was *unübersichtlich* in real time. Rather like Eratosthenes, Redfield
was his own network: he could cross-cut in memory. After gathering more data, including discussions with sailors, he reconstructed
the storm ten years later in an 1831 journal article (Redfield 1831).
His doctrine was the circular motion of storms; hurricanes were
like big tornadoes. The piece ends with an appeal that anyone
possessing additional facts should "leave a memorandum" with
hydrographers Edmund and George Blunt in New York City, sellers
of nautical books and charts (51). Redfield shows the centrality of
the postal system to eighteenth and nineteenth century meanwhile
structures, a critical nationalist medium of imagining untouched by
Anderson, but Redfield also shows that one observer can produce
their own meanwhile—rather like a novelist or a journalist.

One critic thought Redfield's inability to prove tight synchronization was his Achilles' heel: the trees could have been flattened by a different or later storm two or three days later (Mitchell 1831, 362). Such is the eternal threat to retrospectively inferred simultaneity: the risk that indeterminate time lags confound the data. Only as the electrical telegraph provided weather data in more or less real time were same-day weather reports possible. This was a boutique genre in the 1850s and a fledgling journalistic genre in the 1860s, in the United States and United Kingdom at least. The telegraph enabled the separation of communication and transportation for the first time in history, says James Carey (1989). That may be, but the telegraph also did something else: it separated weather from climate for the first time! Climate lasts weeks, months, seasons, or years: weather is daily. Brandes reconstructed the weather of 1783 in 1816; Redfield of 1821 in 1831; James Pollard Espy analyzed a June 20, 1836, storm in an 1837 report. The amount of time that it took to cover space was shrinking.

The Demons of Microtime

Just as the telegraph made instantaneous communication possible, thoughtful souls discovered its bondage to the Hare principle. Electricity travels at the speed of light—and the speed of light is finite. Even the fastest transmissions cannot exceed 300,000 km/sec. On a cosmic scale, this is not fast enough to create a central grid of time coordination. The telegraph enabled superfast transmissions and also disclosed the older regime of a universe of asynchrony. This is the discovery of Einstein (Galison 2003).

The between-time is a time for mischief of all kinds, as well as of monopolies of knowledge. The novelist can track between characters. Mathematicians and evangelists can dramatically join separate events. Young meteorologists can read storm patterns they could not have witnessed for themselves. The stock market now operates in microseconds and even nanoseconds, thanks to high-frequency trading. Paul Baran's supposedly innocent plan for

a network based on the microtimes of packet switching has created
a system in which every node could potentially access the whole
network, in which every split second was the strait gate through
which the spies and hackers could enter (Sprenger 2015). Blind-
ness to the arts of buffering time has cost us all dearly. Oblivious
simultaneity is written into our condition, but critical analysis helps
us see that synchronization always takes time, affects space, and
consumes energy or power.

Notes

I am grateful to the Center for Advanced Studies in Oslo for giving me time and space to write this piece. I thank Helge Jordheim and Espen Ytreberg for friendship, hospitality, and commentary.

1   Anderson mentions *The Gutenberg Galaxy* with a brisk brush-off (34n58), but
    see McLuhan (1952). "The new book of the people, the newspaper, created a
    one-day world utterly indifferent to the past, but embracing the whole planet.
    The newspaper is not a time-binder but a space-binder. Juxtaposed simultane-
    ously in its columns are events from the next block with events from China and
    Peru." A newspaper "surrealistically" collects its items under the rigid "conven-
    tion of a single date-line."
2   Thanks to Mary J. Depew for guidance on Homer.
3   This custom is based in the Hebrew Bible and is developed in the Mishnah's
    section on festivals (Moed).
4   A helpful collection of sources and more recent discussions of the doubling
    of the "yom tov" (holiday) is http://www.michaelbrochstein.com/misc/Second
    DayYomTov.htm.
5   Aristotle, *Politics,* book 3, part 3, trans. Jowett, http://classics.mit.edu/Aristotle/
    politics.3.three.html.
6   Personal communication, June 22, 2019.
7   See https ://en.wikipedia.org/wiki/Shuidiao_Getou 千里共嬋娟. Personal com-
    munication, Su Hua, June 15, 2019.
8   Richard Francis Burton, trans., *The Book of a Thousand Nights and a Night* (1887),
    vol. 13 https://en.wikisource.org/wiki/The_Book_of_the_Thousand_Nights_and
    _a_Night/Volume_13.
9   The work of my colleague Deborah Coen is essential; see Coen (2018).

References

Anderson, Benedict. 1983. *Imagined Communities: Reflections on the Origin and Spread of Nationalism.* London: Verso.

50 Anderson, Benedict. 1998. *Spectre of Comparisons*. London: Verso.

Auerbach, Erich. 1953. *Mimesis,* trans. Willard R. Trask. Princeton, N.J.: Princeton University Press.

Bacon, Francis. 1844. *Works of Francis Bacon,* ed. Basil Montagu, 3 vols. Philadelphia: Carey and Hart.

Brandes, F. W. 1819. "Einige Resultate aus der Witterungs-Geschichte des Jahres 1783, und Bitte um Nachrichten aus jener Zeit; aus einem Schreiben des Professor Brandes an Gilbert." *Annalen der Physik* 61:621–26.

Brandes, F. W. 1820. *Beiträge zur Witterungskunde*. Leipzig: Johannes Ambrosius Barth.

Bynner, Witter. 1982. The Chinese Translations. New York: Farrar, Straus, Giroux.

Carey, James W. 1989. "Technology and Ideology: The Case of the Telegraph," In *Communication as Culture: Essays on Media and Society,* 201–30. Boston: Unwin Hyman.

Coen, Deborah. 2018. *Climate in Motion: Science, Empire, and the Problem of Scale*. Chicago: University of Chicago Press.

Culler, Jonathan. 1999. "Anderson and the Novel," *Diacritics* 29, no. 4: 19–39.

Engels, Donald. 1985. "The Length of Eratosthenes' Stade," *The American Journal of Philology* 106, no. 3: 298–311.

Fuller, Lois K. (2006). "The 'Genitive Absolute' in New Testament/Hellenistic Greek: A Proposal for Clearer Understanding," *Journal of Greco-Roman Christianity and Judaism* 3:142–67.

Galison, Peter. 2003. *Einstein's Clocks, Poincaré's Maps: Empires of Time*. New York: Norton.

Girard, Réné. 1961. *Mensonge romantique et vérité romanesque*. Paris: Grasset.

Kittler, Friedrich. 2003. "Blitz und Serie—Ereignis und Donner." In *Ereignis: Eine fundamentale Kategorie der Zeiterfahrung Anspruch und Aporien,* ed. Nikolaus Müller-Schöll, 145–58. Bielefeld: Transcript.

McLuhan, Marshall. 1952. "Technology and Political Change," *International Journal* 3:189–95.

Mitchell, Elisha. 1831. "On Storms and Meteorological Observations," *American Journal of Science and Arts* 20:361–369.

Monmonier, Mark. 1999. *Air Apparent: How Meteorologists Learned to Map, Predict, and Dramatize Weather*. Chicago: University of Chicago Press.

Redfield, William C. 1831. "Remarks on the Prevailing Storms of the Atlantic Coast, of the North American States," *American Journal of Science and Arts* 20:17–51.

Ryan, Mark. 2016. *Geometry for Dummies,* 3rd. ed. Hoboken, N.J.: Wiley.

Scodel, Ruth. 2008. "Zielinski's Law Reconsidered," *Transactions of the American Philological Association* 138:107–25.

Siegert, Bernhard. 2015. "Longitude and Simultaneity in Philosophy, Physics, and Empires," *Configurations* 23:145–63.

Sprenger, Florian. 2015. *The Politics of Micro-Decisions: Edward Snowden, Net Neutrality, and the Architectures of the Internet,* trans. Valentin Pakis. Lüneburg: Meson Press.

Winkler, Hartmut. 2009. "Geometry of Time: Media, Spatialization, and Reversibility." http://homepages.uni-paderborn.de/winkler/hase_e.pdf.

Winkler, Hartmut. 2015. *Prozessieren: Die dritte, vernachlässigte Medienfunktion*. Paderborn: Wilhelm Fink.

Physics and Aesthetics: Simulation as Action at a Distance

Christina Vagt

In today's material science, "spooky" *action at a distance* has no place. When an Australian banksia tree suddenly opens the follicles of its cones to release its seeds in the aftermath of a wildfire, cause and effect are evident to the careful observer: The fire gets rid of the competition. But the sheer fact that the cone, which has been technically dead for a decade, can actually perform this kind of specific and goal-oriented motion does appear strange—until experiments in combination with imaging and modeling techniques finally enable scientists to procure a viable model that can not only simulate the opening process of the follicles but also explain its material structure in detail. The role of computer models for this kind of material research is crucial because it mediates not only between theory and data but also (re-)directs the research itself. By discussing two experimental systems from the field of biomaterial research in terms of aesthetic theories, this essay pursues two strategies: to demonstrate how the mediation between experimental and simulated data codetermines whether a viable model of a biomaterial structure can ever be procured, and second, to understand scientific computer models themselves as aesthetic procedures that create their own specific objects of study

["*Anschauungsobjekte*"], therefore extending the media question underlying natural sciences into the realm of digital technologies. Computer simulations belong to a long history of action at a distance through models but also through concepts, and the question they raise does not concern causality and instantaneity so much as the relation between living processes and their mathematical conceptualization.

Computer Simulations with Blumenberg

Recent decades have produced a growing number of publications on the history and epistemology of computer simulations within the history of science, media studies, and philosophy of science. Peter Galison describes the coming of computer simulations as a new and interdisciplinary way to conduct science beyond the traditional distinction of theory and experiment. Beginning with historic computer simulations that led to the design of the first hydrogen bomb in 1952, computer simulations changed the status of the computer within science and engineering from "computer-as-tool to computer-as-nature" (Galison 2011, 121). Paul Edwards states that, during the Cold War, simulations had "more political significance and more cultural influence than the weapons that could not be used" (Edwards 1997, 14). Claus Pias (2011) demonstrates the rootedness of computer simulations in so-called mode-two sciences that operate in a problem-oriented, contextualized, and multidisciplinary fashion. They produce second-order statistics that can model the behavior of systems within complex environmental interactions, and, as a political technology, they belong to preventive risk-managing strategies of governance. Eric Winsberg (2003) argues that techniques of simulation, like experiments, have a life of their own and carry their own credentials. Meanwhile, Till Grüne-Yanoff and Paul Weirich (2010) refer to the flexible distinction between computer models and simulations, while providing a useful overview of the scientific use of simulations that might function as proof, projection, explanation, or policy formulation. Last but not least, Gabriele Gramelsberger stresses the role that computer simulations play in sciences without "first principles," such as life sciences, neurosciences, and climatology and their role for sociopolitical practices that rely heavily on models (Gramelsberger 2011). She also relates computer simulations to textual narrations in fiction, such as a short story, novella, or detective story. Like literature, computer simulations apply different temporalities, and the temporality of the plot is not identical with the time of the plot (Gramelsberger 2008).

The following essay builds on this historic and epistemological research, while stressing the role that *aesthetic procedures* play for computer models and pursuing the hypothesis that computer simulations are aesthetic procedures in and of themselves, because they create their objects of study—they make things appear that weren't known before. The starting point for this inquiry into the interaction of technology and aesthetics are two experimental systems in the field of biomaterial research, which investigates structural mechanics performed by animals and plants. The role of imaging technologies for computer models in biomaterial research was obvious from the start, yet, through observations and discussions with the involved scientists and engineers over the period of one year, it also became clear that the models redirect the imaging process. This "loop" between scientists and modelers (Gramelsberger 2008) gave rise to my own research on the function of aesthetics for concepts of matter, because it raised questions about the influence of design [*Formgebung*] on the conceptualization of biomaterials and living matter.

To mobilize aesthetic theories in order to understand the role of imaging and modeling technologies in material sciences might seem an awkward approach—to scientists and engineers, at least, who usually think of them as tools. What this aesthetic discussion provides is insight into the reality claims of both the model and the modeled object, something that is rarely discussed in science and engineering but is nevertheless crucial when it comes to discussing the outcomes of scientific research with a broader public, especially when modeling plays a central role in politics and policy making. The experimental setup of these systems, which constantly trade first- and second-order data, allows for a "close reading" of the modeling process itself. Even though no immediate political or ethical questions implied in the research will be discussed here, understanding how imaging and simulation techniques bridge the gap between classic experiments and computer models might also provide insight into how to read more complicated models in which the mediation between object and model cannot be as easily followed, as is the case with climate models (see Oreskes, Stainforth, and Smith 2010).

Within their respective experimental systems, computer simulations define living matter as scientific objects in terms of the "space of possibility," a term borrowed from Michel Serres, who borrowed it from Robert Musil (see Serres 1978). The computer model defines the probabilistic realm that restricts possible data values and behavior—both experimentally and virtually. This highly dynamic space that—unlike the classic spaces associated with Newtonian mechanics or Euclidean geometry—is not fixed once and for all, but rather its actuality depends on its ability to simulate the behavior of the material under specific conditions. And while the model is being used to simulate behavior under variable conditions, it is itself subject to modifications by the modeler. As an epistemological technology, i.e. a knowledge-generating technology, computer simulations are themselves the outcome of a new statistical concept of matter that started with thermodynamics and electrodynamics and was eventually formalized in nuclear and quantum physics during the first half of the twentieth century. According to quantum physics, matter is conceived as being both discrete and continuous but more importantly as dynamic, since it exchanges energy with its environments. It even defines certain properties of time and space rather than being submerged to fixed space coordinates. Not only does matter stop being passive and inert, it also gives rise to new means of manipulation and technology design. When John von Neumann and Stanislav Ulam designed the first computer model, it happened in the attempt to solve the almost unsolvable problem of how to design a hydrogen bomb. How can one build a weapon whose physical properties were not understood in detail and that, furthermore, couldn't be subjected to classic experimentation either, because the forces and temperatures involved were too destructive to be tried out under laboratory conditions? Over the course of the twentieth century, simulating something that cannot be tested under real-world conditions became the new third category added to the former scientific duality of theory and experiment, according to Galison (see Galison 2005). This "third way" of simulation became particularly productive in engineering. Largely overlooked, however, has been that any procedure for making things appear to the senses—making things appear where they are not, or rather before they actually come into being—is an aesthetic procedure.

When computer simulations are part of complex experimental systems involving different kinds of measuring and imaging techniques, they mediate between image and model. This process cannot be entirely reduced to semantic or logical terms. It is in fact an aesthetic procedure in the sense of designed sensual cognition [*gestaltete sinnliche Erkenntnis*], whose outcome depends on the potential and quality of the measuring and imaging techniques that are applied, as well as the design of the model. In this sense, computer simulations themselves can be understood as an aesthetic procedure that requires, like any other aesthetic procedure in literature or art, a certain temporal and spatial distance to real-world phenomena of the living environment and its corporeal and tactile information. In today's scientific cultures, computer simulations are a prominent type of action at a distance, a classic concept of agency that does not exclusively refer to physical phenomena, such as electromagnetism or gravitation, but also to cognition. According to Hans Blumenberg, action at a distance signifies physical as well as cognitive processes, and cognition always implies sensual data and therefore aesthetics (see Blumenberg and Haverkamp 2010). The ability to act from a spatial and temporal distance, to act on something *in absentia,* is not exclusive to humans—after all, the sun acts on the earth from quite a distance—but it does characterize human agency to a large degree. For Blumenberg, human action is characterized by an "ontological distance between an object of knowledge and its knower" (Blumenberg and Hawkins 2015, 156). Conceptuality is grounded in this type of remote agency: A *Begriff,* a notion or concept, is an action that implies the absence of the object. The German notion for "notion"—*Begriff*—implies *greifen,* which can be translated as "to grasp," "to grab," or "to seize," as does the English notion "concept," a calque from Latin *"concipio"* or *"con"* (with) + "capio," where *capio* means "to capture," "to seize," or "to take." Concepts have to be vague enough to encompass the boundaries of a thing and yet leave enough room for any concrete perception still to come along. Concepts act like a mesh for future sensations, they are a form of preemptive action, which Blumenberg imagines to have started in prehistoric times with the throwing of a spear or the setting of a trap. Preemptive behavior exists in all human societies, at work in hunter-gatherer cultures as well as in European philosophies of mind, matter, and life. Concepts as preemptive behavior are not simply based on objects—as a fact, the former constitutes the latter. According to Kant, this is particularly valid for mathematical terms; according to Freud this is true for the notion of the unconscious; and according to Leibniz, it also applies to playing music, a mental power of computation without the awareness that one is generating numbers. Mathematics, the unconscious, music—these are three very diverse realms that nevertheless are driven by objects that are themselves generated by concepts. In a more general sense, Blumenberg implies that they provide a particular insight into the structure of human reason, which is another example of an object generated by concepts. Human reason as the sum of conceptuality relies on action at distance, on the aesthetic intermediation between concepts and objects. Computer simulations therefore belong to the history of action at a distance through notions and reason, they are a type of symbolic labor [*Arbeit am Begriff*] with real-world consequences. And just as concepts and reason evolve through aesthetic processes involving metaphoric, metonymic, and contingent elements, computer simulations—even

though mathematical in nature—depend on experimental data,
pattern recognition, and design [*Formgebung*].

The two experimental biomaterial systems that are discussed here serve as close readings of engineering methods applied within the life sciences. They demonstrate how matter and life are converging within the modeling process, and how imaging and modeling techniques bridge the gap between these formerly distinct orders. Of primary interest here are not the scientific outcomes but the modeling process itself, how it can be better understood within the intertwined histories of aesthetics and matter, and how it can inform media-theoretical discussions on matter and materiality.

Imaging Tunicates

Tunicates, in Latin *oikopleura dioica,* are tiny marine animals almost invisible to the human eye. As part of the zooplankton, they inhabit the upper, warmer layers of the world's oceans, especially coastal waters (Scripps Institute 2019). Their specialty is that they unfold a "house" or "body housing," also described as "filtering mechanism" that enables the animal to filter the sea water for digestible algae and transports it into the mouth of the animal (see Jany und Razghandi, forthcoming). A research group at Humboldt University in Berlin and the Max Planck Institute for Material Science in Potsdam under the leadership of biologist Thomas Stach investigates the anatomical mechanism that unfolds the house. In order to study the filtering and unfolding operations of the house, they are attempting to build a computer model of the organism in order to eventually be able to simulate the unfolding process of the house as a whole and to find answers to the leading question: Is there a specific design, a biomaterial design, that enables the tunicate to unfold its complex cellulose house approximately every four hours during its short lifespan of seven days?

After slicing the material and taking single microscopic images, thousands of slices have to be reassembled both manually and

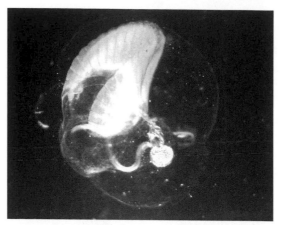

[Figure 3.1]. Microscopic image of a living tunicate inside its "house." The head of the animal is dyed yellow and orange, parts of the house are already filled with undigestible purple-dyed plant particles. Image courtesy of Khashayar Razghandi.

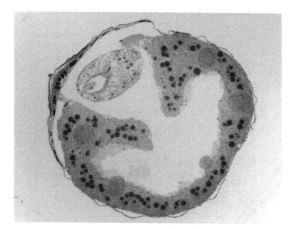

[Figure 3.2]. As with most biological research, it starts with microscopy. The animal body or biomaterial is cut into ultrathin slices, each only a couple of hundred nanometers thick, and each microscopic image is digitally captured. Image courtesy of Khashayar Razghandi and Thomas Stach; produced in the laboratory of Thomas Stach (Humboldt University, Berlin, Comparative Electronmicroscopy).

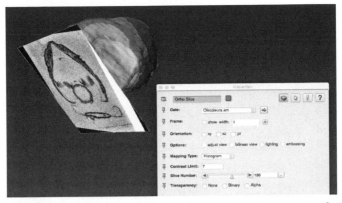

[Figure 3.3]. A 3D model is then built from the microscopic images. Image courtesy of Khashayar Razghandi and Thomas Stach; produced in the laboratory of Thomas Stach (Humboldt University, Berlin, Comparative Electronmicroscopy).

through software into a three-dimensional model, which is then able to generate parameters to create a second model that can be used to run computer simulations on the material.

There are also non-invasive imaging methods that try to capture the living animal in water. The high-resolution images and two-minute-long microscopic film sequences that are produced grant insight into the motoric skills of plankton. The animals drift directionless, absorbing algae. Their movements are characterized through the pulsating rhythm of their beating tails, and the different degrees of liquidity and firmness, translucence and opacity, create the ambience of a floating dance. Beautiful without question, it is difficult to capture on microscopic film the exact moment when the animal unfolds a new house. Stach's group has not been able to realize a computer model on the basis of this imagery. There were simply not enough viable data. Among the difficulties of the modeling process lies life itself. Technologies such as Raman spectroscopy and electron microscopy often help to identify the distribution of biochemical components and structural organization within biomaterials, but the biomaterial has to be

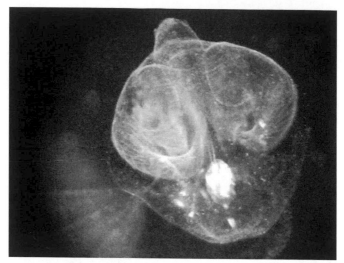

[Figure 3.4]. Still image from a microscopic film, with a cloud of orange-dyed algae that the animal will start feeding on soon. After a couple of hours of eating and filtering, the house is completely opaque and congested. The animal leaves its house behind, and after a couple of hours and unfolds a new one. Image courtesy of Khashayar Razghandi.

"prepared" in order to employ such technologies, a highly technical process that is also deadly for the animal. The paradox of these efficient measuring and imaging techniques lies in the fact that they cannot be performed on living organisms, and a dead animal can no longer perform the unfolding mechanism.

Biomaterials with Bergson and Schrödinger

This paradoxical relation between living motion and its visual and conceptual representations lies at the core of science and philosophy—at least in the view of French philosopher Henri Bergson, who calls it the "cinematographic mechanism" of the human intellect. It signifies a fundamental shortcoming of perception, intellect, and language: Humans perceive, recognize, and verbalize motion by looking at it from the outside, as a succession of discrete states or forms. In science and engineering, this leads to the idea of motion as being sprawled out within a Cartesian coordinate system, allowing for its translation into algebraic formula and calculation (see Bergson 1908, 295–375). The cinematographic mechanism is probably the most quoted Bergsonian metaphor, ever since Gilles Deleuze based his cinema theory on it. But beyond its historic epistemology of chrono-photography and cinema and in an even more general sense, Bergson used it as metaphor for human cognition as a mode of simulation.

The mechanism that simulates continuous motion by moving a succession of still images at a rate that escapes the human eye is a technical concretization of the relation between intellect and matter—at work in our everyday perceptions just as in the measuring sciences. Bergson never seems to get weary of pointing out this blind spot in European philosophy, tracing it from ancient Greece to modern physics of the early twentieth century, following the succession of paradoxes on motion and time. The deficiencies of language are not the point of origin for this blind spot, nor does it lie in the mathematical worldview of scientists. Rather, the cinematographic mechanism points to Bergson's anthropological conception within the structure of the universe itself. It is a necessary intellectual and scientific self-deceiving mechanism that results from what one might call the *will to conceptualization or abstraction* from a concrete situation or object that lies at the bottom of both image- and language-creating processes—Nietzsche calls it the "will to metaphor." It is not restricted to a specific media-technological apparatus; the apparatus simply demonstrates or concretizes the general act of human cognition, which can only deal with real processes and their perceptual data in their absence, by simulating them: Every continuous motion, be it that of light or that of one's own arm, is dissected into discrete sections only to be artificially reanimated into a perceivable motion. European thought has been confusing processes of becoming with the successions of forms right from the beginning, from Platonism onward. According to Bergson's judgment, both science and philosophy are based on this self-concealing mechanism. But while science needs to adhere to it as best it can, philosophy needs to reveal it in order to illuminate the mind's constant simulation of motion, which permits—through distance—different, more complex forms of behavior and action. When it comes to simulation, science and philosophy seem to work in opposite directions. This division of labor becomes particularly clear when Bergson elaborates on the history of matter: Most physicists before 1900 and the advent of special relativity theory treated solid matter as if it were identical to geometry, following a concept of passive matter inherited from Descartes and the technique of analytical geometry culminating in Newtonian mechanics. From a historical perspective, the task of physics has been to push representations of matter virtually toward the direction of space, because matter and human intellect (which is itself immersed in a material universe) alike have a natural affinity for space and geometry; matter and intellect share a certain degree of inertia, so to say. As a result, physics before the nineteenth century ignored the temporal aspect of the material universe, the fact that it is immersed in processes of evolution and becoming (see Bergson 1944, 216). Bergson sees the reason for this geometrical bias, this geometrical inclination of science, in the structure of the universe itself: Everything that exists, including matter, is subjected to processes of temporal change and becoming but can only appear to the senses because it is embedded in matter. Science has to overlook the fact that it deals with life only in terms of the cinematographic mechanism, that it has to simulate an object in order to learn anything about it. According to Bergson, concepts of science are but symbolic or visual simulations, mathematical notations, aesthetical procedures, and they could have turned out in many different ways. But even though they are never inevitable or determined, they also did not evolve by pure chance, otherwise science would not have progressed:

> And yet there is an order approximately mathematical immanent in matter, an objective order, which our science approaches in proportion to progress. [. . .] It is true that

laws of mathematical form will never apply to it completely. For that, it would have to become pure space and step
out of duration. (Bergson 1944, 218)

Matter appears to be subjected to change and becoming, and at
the same time it has a tendency toward the rigor of geometric
relations. It is extended between two poles, one of pure space
and one of pure becoming, but it will never entirely coincide or
converge with either one of them. The artificial or human aspect
of modern science is not the geometrical bias itself but rather the
need to measure, which paradoxically generates its success:

In a general way, measuring is a wholly human operation,
which implies that we really or ideally superpose two objects a certain number of times. Nature did not dream of
this superposition. It does not measure, nor does it count.
Yet physics counts, measures, relates "quantitative" varia-
tions to one another to obtain laws, and it succeeds. (218)

Against the background of evolutionary theory, Bergson concludes
that mathematical order is in itself not factual or real but simply
"the form toward which a certain interruption tends of itself, and
that materiality consists precisely of an interruption of this kind"
(219). Lacking the modern concept of information, Bergson strug-
gles to explain how mathematics introduces negativity into matter,
and how this solely serves a communicative, social function: "Negation, therefore, differs from affirmation properly so called in that it
is an affirmation of the second degree: it affirms something of an
affirmation which itself affirms something of an object" (288).

If negation is a process that takes place in time, it is primarily a
temporal and not a logical operation and immanent in all material
processes. With this understanding of mathematics as a symbolic
and socially determined type of interaction with material processes
of change and becoming, there is no need to assume a presta-
bilized harmony between mathematics and the world, because
their relation—being social and communicative in nature—is not

determined but contingent to a certain degree, just like the relation between actuality and formalism in philosophical systems, spoken or formal languages, social organization, and so on.

> And yet it [mathematics, CV] succeeds, just because there is no definite system of mathematical laws, at the base of nature, and because mathematics in general represents simply the side to which matter inclines. [. . .] we can take matter by any end and handle it in any way, it will always fall back into some one of our mathematical formulae, because it is weighed with geometry. (219)

Life and matter are two different motions bound to interrupt each other. In its most extreme forms, matter almost exhibits purely geometrical, mechanistic behavior—that is why Bergson sometimes refers to it as the "automatic" or "inert order"—a pretty adequate description of what physics nowadays calls the stillness that befalls quantum systems near absolute zero. Matter near absolute zero does not allow for life, because the living is weighted with becoming and subject to constant change. Transformation cannot happen without matter, matter would not exist without transformation: "Things and states are only views, taken by our mind, of becoming. There are not things, there are only actions" (248). Over the course of the history of Western sciences and their media technologies that measure motion, matter seems to be on its way toward mathematics. In the late 1930s, at the end of Bergson's lifespan, which saw the coming of relativity theory and quantum mechanics and the settlement of the mathematical *Grundlagenstreit* through Gödel's *Entscheidungstheorem,* matter and mathematics really do seem to converge. But according to Bergson's prognosis, even though the latest matter models come very close to being completely mathematized, they will never completely coincide, not because of faulty science or mathematics but rather because matter is also subjected to becoming and life. Life and matter are inverse and continuous movements that interrupt (or discretize) each other.

> In reality, life is a movement, materiality is the inverse
> movement, and each of these two movements is simple,
> the matter which forms a world being an undivided flux,
> and undivided also the life that runs through it, cutting
> out in it living beings all along its track. (249)

Together but in opposite directions, life and matter are part of the
same real process, while both human cognition and science can
only account for the result of their interaction, namely the cut-out
forms of living beings. Bergson's image of an "undivided flux of
matter" follows the energetic model of late nineteenth-century
thermodynamics and its second law, stating that matter, if left
alone, has a tendency toward equal distribution. While matter is
subject to the time arrow of entropy, living beings seem to be able
to hold off this process of thermodynamic equal distribution (or
death) during their lifespan. An organism is able, for as long as it
stays alive, to withstand the second law of thermodynamics and
decrease the amount of entropy by interacting with its environment. Bergson understands this counterforce to entropy as a vital
force [*élan vital*] (268). Quantum physicist Erwin Schrödinger states
the problem in a very similar manner in his book *What Is Life?*,
which resulted from a series of public lectures in 1943. Schrödinger
explores, like Bergson, the threshold between physics and biology,
but instead of using Bergson's vitalist term *élan vital*, Schrödinger
invents the concept of "negative entropy":

> Every process, event, happening—call it what you will; in
> a word, everything that is going on in Nature means an
> increase of the entropy of the part of the world where it is
> going on. Thus a living organism continually increases its
> entropy—or, as you may say, produces positive entropy—
> and thus tends to approach the dangerous state of maxi-
> mum entropy, which is death. It can only keep aloof from
> it, i.e. alive, by continually drawing from its environment
> negative entropy—which is something very positive as we
> shall immediately see. What an organism feeds upon is

negative entropy. Or, to put it less paradoxically, the essential thing in metabolism is that the organism succeeds in freeing itself from all the entropy it cannot help producing while alive. (Schrödinger 1992, 71)

Living matter is able to keep entropy, aka death, at bay by absorbing negative entropy from its environment. Schrödinger did not receive much praise from the scientific community for his neologism, apparently translating the order of the living organism into the order of computable matter did not help. In a rhetorical move, Schrödinger both introduces and abandons the concept in *What Is Life*, and introduces instead—for the first time in the history of science—the concept of a genetic code. The rhetoric of *What Is Life?* and the emergence of the concept of a genetic code are remarkable, because unlike negative entropy, it has made an almost unprecedented career as a scientific concept within the life sciences over the course of the twentieth and twenty-first centuries. Revisiting Schrödinger's disputed and now outdated concept of negative entropy is nevertheless insightful, because it differentiates between the computability of matter and the organization of life, a distinction that the notion of the genetic code effaces (Weigel 2006). Schrödinger and Bergson were convinced that the two orders of life and matter cannot be converted into one, because they are complementary to each other. If they ever converge, it would mean the end of time and life. Their insight, that life and matter, living matter, is not just governed by a single movement but by two (because their movements are essentially inverse or negative toward each other, a form of difference or interruption) effectively gets lost in the models of cybernetics and information theory that succeeded them. But the practical obstacles in building computer models of living matter again brings the two-fold aspect of living matter to the fore: When modeling dynamic or living processes, organized and coded processes, both movements have to be taken into account: the tendency of matter toward geometry and its interference with immanent becoming. And the problems of imaging and data analysis do not stop once and for all, indeed they carry on into the actual building of the model itself.

Our second experimental system of biomaterial investigates the opening mechanism of follicles of *Banksia attenuate.* Banksia plants come in diverse sizes and shapes of trees and bushes, and among botanists they are famous for their seed pods. These cones are technically "dead" or "inanimate" because they no longer participate in the active metabolism of the plant, but they nevertheless are able to open after being exposed to the extreme environmental conditions of a wildfire.

Its opening mechanism enables this species, endemic to Australia, to compete with other trees. The research group of Michaela Eder at the Max Planck Institute of Colloids and Interfaces in Potsdam is building a computer model that allows them to run computer simulations of this opening mechanism. The model is an example of the standard computer simulation for structural analysis of solid matter and for the design of such, e.g. for airplane and automobile designs, the so-called Finite Element Method (FEM) (see Clough 2004). FEM is one of the most common types of computer simulations in and outside science today. It has a vast distribution among industrial engineering fields as well as in material science. Many disciplines use it to simulate the behavior of solid-state bodies under fluctuating environmental conditions such as physical impact, air temperature, and so on.

[Figure 3.5]. Banksia pods. After a wildfire, the pods suddenly open their lips and release the seeds. Image by the author.

Every FEM starts with defining the investigated object (and its model) in terms of computer mathematics and the governing physical and chemical laws—including Newtonian laws of motion, the fundamental equilibrium equations of solid mechanics, and the thermodynamic laws for the conversation of energy and increasing entropy—that mark the boundary conditions for every possible motion: its space of possibility. The virtual model has to comply with the same natural laws that govern the properties of the actual body, but, unlike the real banksia pod, the numeric model can only deal with discrete states and a finite set of elements. Therefore, the material continuum of the solid object has to be transformed into groups of finite numbers of discrete elements. One of the first decisions the modeler has to make, then, is what kind of mesh should be applied to describe the body as a network of joint points: If the mesh is too wide, the virtual system will be unstable, and, if it is too fine, the computer will take forever to run the simulations. After defining all mechanical-mathematical conditions and laws

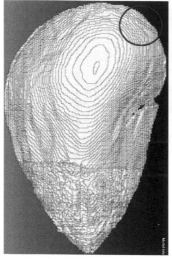

[Figure 3.6]. An important step in building the model is the segmentation of the continuous object into discrete elements. Image courtesy of Huynh Nguyen.

of the model, one needs experimental data from the object under investigation.

Every computer model in biomaterials starts with imaging, and in this case the raw data do not stem from microscopy but from computer tomography scans of the pod in different stages of the opening process. This experimental system has the huge advantage over the tunicate experiment in that the opening process can easily be captured by the imaging technology, e.g. by exposing the pod to wildfire temperatures inside a CT scanner until it opens its lips.

It is also quite convenient that CT and MRI already produce 3D images, therefore they do not have to be aligned like laser sheet microscopies. But they do come in a continuous, analog data form, therefore they have to be segmented before they can be fed into the computer model in the form of discrete mathematics. There would be no computer models in biomaterial research without the countless media technologies of data analysis: from simple microscopic films and photograms to x-rays, CTs, and MRIs, electron microscopies, cryo-electron microscopies, and so forth.

Once a viable computer model has been built, the scientists run simulations on different environmental parameters. The model is constantly revised in the process of simulation and further experimentation on the mechanical and biochemical qualities and properties of the pods. Through this interplay or loop between simulation runs and real-world data analysis, the behavior of the biomaterial and its mathematical model do indeed converge.

In comparison, the two experimental systems point out the difficulties in building a viable computer model of living matter. We also see that the FEM method much better serves to simulate the structural motion of inanimate matter. The obstacles for analyzing the unfolding of the tunicate already start with imaging—it is quite difficult to gather experimental data when it is impossible to perform electron-microscopy on the material. The movements that would describe the unfolding of the tunicate's house seem

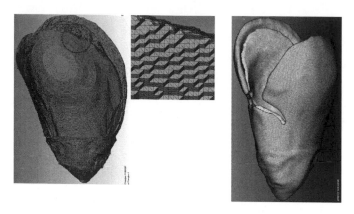

[Figure 3.7]. Meshing of the smooth surface. Image courtesy of Huynh Nguyen.

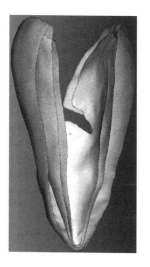

[Figure 3.8]. A first FEM model of the pod. Image courtesy of Huynh Nguyen.

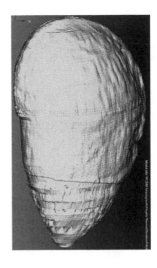

[Figure 3.9]. Validating the experimental data, the model converges with the experimentally minded data. The term "convergence" refers to the state when the model can finally be used to analyze the actual movement of the cone and predict its behavior according to changing environmental factors like temperature, humidity, etc. Image courtesy of Huynh Nguyen.

to be much more complex than those of the banksia pods. The unfolding of the tunicate house transgresses the borders between one, two, and three dimensions, and the unfolding motion of the fragile cellulose houses probably would have been better described in terms of fluid dynamics, since this takes place in water. By running simulations of the banksia opening mechanism, the model has falsified earlier assumptions about the material structures of the follicles. Searching for experimental evidence, a new set of spectroscopies and 3D images was produced, and eventually the opening mechanism was described in a satisfying way (Huss et al. 2017). These research projects count as basic research [*Grundlagenforschung*], and accordingly the models do not have any design applications. It is obvious, however, that the temperature-sensitive mechanism built or coded into the structure of the Banksia pods could enable further research on how plants deal with wildfires and could very well lead to new bio-inspired designs in industry and architecture.

Computer simulations are able to deal with materials by focusing on patterns and structures instead of substances and qualities—they are entirely ignorant of whether or not they model the behavior of tunicates, banksia, or auto bodies. Their ability to abstract from the immediate impressions of sensual data and their focus on the mathematized functions and possible behaviors of a biomaterial is what makes them so valuable at the interface of science and industry. Their degree of abstraction—their distance—from any concrete body or organism enables them to determine the space of possibility, even for the most extreme or even impossible environmental conditions. The model deals with the immanent process of becoming in negative terms by excluding and falsifying everything that the material could not become or do. Unlike cinematic simulations, computer models do indeed converge matter and mathematics. Because they are based on thorough discretization and mathematization, however, they can only be applied after a satisfying amount of data has been collected through classic experimentation. It is therefore misleading to speak of computer simulation as dematerialization—they just operate from a distance, in absence of the object, like concepts and numbers.

Computer Simulations between Physics and Aesthetics

Since the discretization of the object can only take place in its absence, action at a distance is a cornerstone in biomaterial science—not despite but because it also depends heavily on the data gathered through close-up measuring and imaging technologies such as photography, spectroscopy, and 3D imaging. Both imaging and modeling are inevitable for the simulation of biomaterials, because they intermediate between measurements of the

actual material and the virtual design of the computer model that
generates second-order data—data gathered through simulations
(Pias 2011). Like cinematography, today's simulation techniques
discretize continuous movements and then add artificial motion,
but the resulting images and films are data visualizations. Instead
of representing past or actual motion, they produce negative maps
that chart impossible motions. Like concepts, their most important
accomplishment lies in their ability to exclude possibilities: The
mapping of possibilities is production of negation (see Blumenberg
and Haverkamp 2010, 75–76). Simulation allows for the recognition
of something that cannot be perceived, measured, or experienced
in any other way. It enables one to discern gaps within the perceived, the measured, the experienced.

Simulations belong to a history of algorithmic images, which are
generated in a symbolic space (see Montaña and Vagt 2018). But
the numerical models they are based on are also derived from experimental data and operate within theories based on natural laws.
Therefore, computer simulations assemble two movements in
different directions: one that follows the spatial, geometrical, and
immanent order of the model and another of impossible states
that are interrupting or rather restricting each other, generated
by the runs of the simulation. In this sense, computer simulations
do indeed take both spatial and temporal motions into account,
something that Bergson, at the beginning of the twentieth century,
reserved for intellectual beings.

This bridging of life and matter in computer simulations relies
equally on physics and aesthetics, the only two inner-worldly
processes that can be called "real," according to Max Bense. While
physics follows the second law of thermodynamics, according to
which the time arrow of increasing entropy describes the world
in the direction of disorder or the probability of maximum equal
distribution, aesthetics can be comprehended as the inverse
movement, segregating instead of blending (Bense 1960, 20). In
Bergson's philosophy of the living, this results in two opposed
academic cultures of science and philosophy. In Bense's computer-

informed aesthetics of physics from the 1960s, aesthetics occupies the place that for Bergson still belonged to vital concepts such as *élan vital* or statistic concepts such as Schrödinger's negative entropy. Both physics and aesthetics have ceased to simply describe the world as given—instead they try to figure out how to change it. Neither imitates nature any longer, rather both create their own objects. The computer with its regime of information and organization does not dissolve the boundaries between physics and aesthetics, or science and art. What it does is relate them closer to each other than they had been for a long time. Since computer simulations do not yield to any defined reality but operate within terms of possibilities and probabilities, attempting to create viable scenarios rather than ontological certainties, and abstaining from determining the actual outcome of single events, they are not mere tools or instruments of science. They are aesthetic instruments that change the perception of reality.

The idea that the texture of reality itself is subject to historic transformations is not new to the humanities, but it seems to be largely absent in scientific discussions. When Blumenberg distinguishes between different types of reality over the course of European history, he points out that, unlike the incontrovertible and instantaneous reality mediated and guaranteed by Christian theology and ontology in medieval and early modern times, modern realities are neither guaranteed nor instantaneous. Instead, they come with "a sort of 'epic' structure, relating to the totality of a world that can never be completed or grasped in its entirety—a world that can be only partially experienced and so can never exclude different contexts of experience which in themselves constitute different worlds" (Blumenberg 1979, 33). Realities do not refer to one nature any longer but require constant actualization and realization. They often take the form of logical paradoxes, something modern physics incorporated like no other scientific discipline. Quantum and relativity physics have been operating with restricted realities for more than one hundred years and they reflect the boundaries of their validity through physical constants. For physics as well as

for aesthetics, reality is a context, a surrounding grammatical or
mathematical structure:

> Reality can no longer be considered an inherent quality of
> an object, but is the embodiment of a consistently applied
> *syntax of elements.* Reality presents itself now as ever
> before as a sort of text which takes on its particular form
> by obeying certain rules of internal consistency. Reality is
> for modern times a context [. . .]. Now, if aesthetic ob-
> jects can have such a thing as a specific reality, they, too,
> are not only bound by the criterion of context as proof
> of their reality but are also constrained, as regards their
> scope and the wealth of elements they incorporate, to
> compete with the context of *Nature,* i.e., to become *sec-
> ondary worlds:* they no longer extract, by imitation, reali-
> ties from the one reality, but imitate the fact of being real.
> (Blumenberg 1979, 42)

Secondary worlds, worlds that imitate the fact of being real, are
simulated worlds. When media theory speaks of computer simulations as artificial nature or world-making technology, it has to take
the interdependence between science and aesthetics into account.
It must do so because not only is there an aesthetic context to
scientific objects, but science also frames aesthetic objects. What
might perhaps be difficult to understand about this relation is the
fact that it disables arguments in terms of causality and instantaneity, because the time arrows of aesthetics and physics do not run
in the same direction. Furthermore, the efficacy of their interaction,
the interdependent calibration, can only be understood through
distance. The virtual model has to be reconfigured in accordance
with real-world data and curves that describe the actual behavior
of the material under certain stress conditions, such as pressure,
temperature, and humidity. Since the computer model is able to
converge the actual and the virtual, as well as matter and mathematics, it can reach a degree of reality that allows experiments to
be conducted within this model. Once a model converges—when
it reaches an adequate degree of reality, so to speak—it serves as

second world or second nature in which mathematical experimentation beyond the limits of actual matter can be conducted. It will never produce certainty; instead it creates new spaces of possibility, be it for the design of new materials according to user and environmental concerns or policy making in regard to phenomena beyond perception, such as climate change. It is not a medium of certainty but of investigation and speculation.

Notes

The idea for this project emerged from interdisciplinary research on self-moving materials at the Cluster of Excellence "Image Knowledge Gestaltung," a joint venture of Humboldt University Berlin and the Max Planck Institute for Colloids and Interfaces in Potsdam. This article would not have been possible without the work and help of Susanne Jany, Khashayar Rhazgandi, Nhu Huynh Nguyen, Michaela Eder, John Dunlop, and Thomas Stach. In addition, I would like to thank Matthias Koch, who introduced me to Blumenberg's concept "actio per distans," and to Jacob Watson for editing this article.

References

Bense, Max. 1960. *Programmierung des Schönen: Allgemeine Texttheorie und Textästhetik*. Baden-Baden: Agis-Verlag.

Bergson, Henri. 1908. "L'evolution creatrice." https://archive.org/details/levolution creatr00berguoft.

Bergson, Henri. 1944. *Creative Evolution,* trans. Arthur Mitchell. New York: Modern Library.

Blumenberg, Hans. 1979. "The Concept of Reality and the Possibility of the Novel." In *New Perspectives in German Literary Criticism*, ed. Richard E. Amacher and Victor Lange, trans. David Henry Wilson. Princeton, N.J.: Princeton University Press.

Blumenberg, Hans., and Anselm Haverkamp. 2010. *Theorie der Unbegrifflichkeit*. Frankfurt am Main: Suhrkamp.

Blumenberg, Hans., and Spencer Hawkins. 2015. *The Laughter of the Thracian Woman: A Protohistory of Theory*. New York: Bloomsbury Academic US.

Clough, R. W. 2004. "Early History of the Finite Element Method from the View Point of a Pioneer." *International Journal for Numerical Methods in Engineering* 60:283–87.

Edwards, Paul N. 1997. *The Closed World: Computers and the Politics of Discourse in Cold War America*. Cambridge, Mass.: MIT Press.

Galison, Peter Louis. 2005. *Image and Logic: A Material Culture of Microphysics*. Chicago; London: University of Chicago Press.

Galison, Peter Louis. 2011. "Computer Simulations and the Trading Zone." In *From*

Science to Computational Science, ed. Gabriele Gramelsberger, 118–57. Zürich: Diaphanes.

Gramelsberger, Gabriele. 2008. "The Epistemic Texture of Simulated Worlds." In *Simulation: Presentation Technique and Cognitive Method,* ed. Andrea Gleiniger and Georg Vrachliotis. Basel-Boston-Berlin: Birkhäuser.

Gramelsberger, Gabriele. 2011. "From Science to Computational Sciences: A Science History and Philosophy Overview." In *From Science to Computational Sciences,* 19–44. Zürich: Diaphanes.

Grüne-Yanoff, Till, und Paul Weirich. 2010. "The Philosohy and Epistemology of Simulation: A Review." *Simulation and Gaming* 41, no. 1: 20–50.

Huss, Jessica C., Vanessa Schoeppler, David J. Merritt, Christine Best, Eric Maire, Jérôme Adrien, Oliver Spaeker, et al. 2017. "Climate-Dependent Heat-Triggered Opening Mechanism of Banksia Seed Pods." *Advanced Science* 5, no. 1: https://doi .org/10.1002/advs.201700572.

Jany, Susanne, and Khashayar Razghandi. Forthcoming. "Filterarchitektur als Modell: Eine interdisziplinäre Auseinandersetzung mit dem Manteltier Oikopleura Dioca." In *Typologie der Hütte.* Zürich: Diaphanes.

Montaña, Ricardo Cedeño, and Christina Vagt. 2018. "Constructing the Invisible— Computer Graphics and the End of Optical Media." *Communication Plus 1* 7, no. 1: Article 2. https://doi.org/10.7275/ksgk-8x88.

Oreskes, Naomi, David Stainforth, and Leonard A. Smith. 2010. "Adaptation to Global Warming: Do Climate Models Tell Us What We Need to Know?" *Philosophy of Science* 77, no. 5: 1012–28.

Pias, Claus. 2011. "On the Epistemology of Computer Simulation." *Zeitschrift für Medien- und Kulturforschung* 1:29–54.

Schrödinger, Erwin. 1992. What Is Life? Cambridge: Cambridge University Press.

Scripps Institute. 2019. "Zooplankton Guide." June 28, 2019. https://scripps.ucsd.edu/ zooplanktonguide/species/oikopleura-dioica.

Serres, Michel. 1978. "Exact and Human." *SubStance* 6, no. 21: 9–19.

Weigel, Sigrid. 2006. *"Die innere Spannung im alpha-numerischen Code" (Flusser): Buchstabe und Zahl in grammatologischer und wissenschaftsgeschichtlicher Perspektive.* Köln: W. König.

Winsberg, Eric. 2003. "Simulated Experiments: Methodology for a Virtual World." *Philosophy of Science* 70:105–25.

Authors

John Durham Peters is the María Rosa Menocal Professor of English and professor of film and media studies at Yale University. He is the author of *Speaking into the Air: A History of the Idea of Communication, Courting the Abyss: Free Speech and the Liberal Tradition,* and most recently Promiscuous Knowledge: Information, Image, and Other Truth Games in History (with the late Kenneth Cmiel).

Florian Sprenger is professor of virtual humanities at Ruhr-Universität Bochum and author of *Politics of Micro-Decisions: Edward Snowden, Net Neutrality, and the Architectures of the Internet.*

Christina Vagt is assistant professor of European media studies in the Department of Germanic and Slavic Studies, University of California, Santa Barbara. She is author of *Geschickte Sprünge: Physik und Medium bei Martin Heidegger.*